THE STORY OF
THE ROMAN PEOPLE

An Elementary History of Rome

BY

EVA MARCH TAPPAN, Ph.D.

Author of "European Hero Stories," "The Story of the Greek People," "American Hero Stories," "Our Country's Story," "England's Story," etc. Editor of " The Children's Hour "

BOSTON, NEW YORK, AND CHICAGO
HOUGHTON MIFFLIN COMPANY
The Riverside Press Cambridge

COPYRIGHT, 1910, BY EVA MARCH TAPPAN

ALL RIGHTS RESERVED

This scarce antiquarian book is included in our special *Legacy Reprint Series*. In the interest of creating a more extensive selection of rare historical book reprints, we have chosen to reproduce this title even though it may possibly have occasional imperfections such as missing and blurred pages, missing text, poor pictures, markings, dark backgrounds and other reproduction issues beyond our control. Because this work is culturally important, we have made it available as a part of our commitment to protecting, preserving and promoting the world's literature. Thank you for your understanding.

BATTLE BETWEEN CONSTANTINE AND MAXENTIUS

PREFACE

THERE is little that is of more practical value to the young folk of to-day than the history of Rome. How a village kingdom became a mighty republic, how the republic became a world-embracing empire, how that empire, the dread and pride of its millions of subjects, fell so low as to become the sport of its own soldiers — all this is, indeed, a tale of marvel. But the history of Rome is more than a mere story. Many of the difficulties and many of the advantages of the Roman Republic are akin to those of the American Republic. The solution of such problems as have already presented themselves in the United States is even now demanding the highest wisdom of the land. Other problems will arise in the near future. Roman history is a mighty object lesson, of value to every citizen of our Republic, of especial value to the children into whose hands the government will so speedily pass. What is learned in years of maturity is an addition to one's mental equipment; what is learned in childhood becomes a part of the mind itself. That those who read this book may find it of interest to-day, of service tomorrow, is the wish of the author.

EVA MARCH TAPPAN.

March 1, 1910.

CONTENTS

THE FIRST PERIOD: ROME AS A KINGDOM

I. THE LEGENDS OF THE SEVEN KINGS OF ROME . . 1
II. THE LEGENDS OF THE SEVEN KINGS OF ROME, *continued* 10

THE SECOND PERIOD: ROME AS A REPUBLIC

III. THE ATTEMPTS OF TARQUINIUS TO REGAIN HIS KINGDOM 25
IV. HOW THE PLEBEIANS WON THEIR RIGHTS . . . 32
V. HOW ROME BECAME RULER OF ITALY 43
VI. THE ROMANS OF THE EARLY REPUBLIC AND THEIR WAYS 61
VII. HOW THE ROMANS CONQUERED CARTHAGE . . . 72
VIII. ROME BECOMES THE CAPITAL OF THE WORLD . . 99
IX. THE GRACCHI; THE RISE OF MARIUS 108
X. THE RULE OF SULLA 123
XI. THE RISE OF POMPEY 136
XII. CÆSAR AND THE TRIUMVIRATES 151

THE THIRD PERIOD: ROME AS AN EMPIRE

XIII. THE REIGN OF AUGUSTUS 169
XIV. THE REST OF THE TWELVE CÆSARS 182
XV. THE FIVE GOOD EMPERORS 200
XVI. FROM MARCUS AURELIUS TO DIOCLETIAN . . . 209
XVII. REIGNS OF DIOCLETIAN AND CONSTANTINE . . . 215
XVIII. THE LAST CENTURIES OF THE EMPIRE . . . 223

IMPORTANT DATES IN ROMAN HISTORY

B. C.

- 753(?) Rome is founded.
- 509 The beginning of the Republic.
- 390 Capture of Rome by the Gauls.
- 266 The whole of Italy is in the hands of Rome.
- 146 Destruction of Carthage.
- 44 Murder of Julius Cæsar.
- 27 Octavianus receives the title of Augustus.

A. D.

- 70 Destruction of Jerusalem.
- 313 The Christians are granted toleration by the Edict of Milan.
- 330 Constantinople becomes the capital of the Empire in the East.
- 395 Division of the Empire.
- 476 The Empire in the West is ruled by a deputy of the Emperor in the East.
- 800 Charlemagne is crowned Emperor of the West.
- 1453 The Turks capture Constantinople.

MAPS

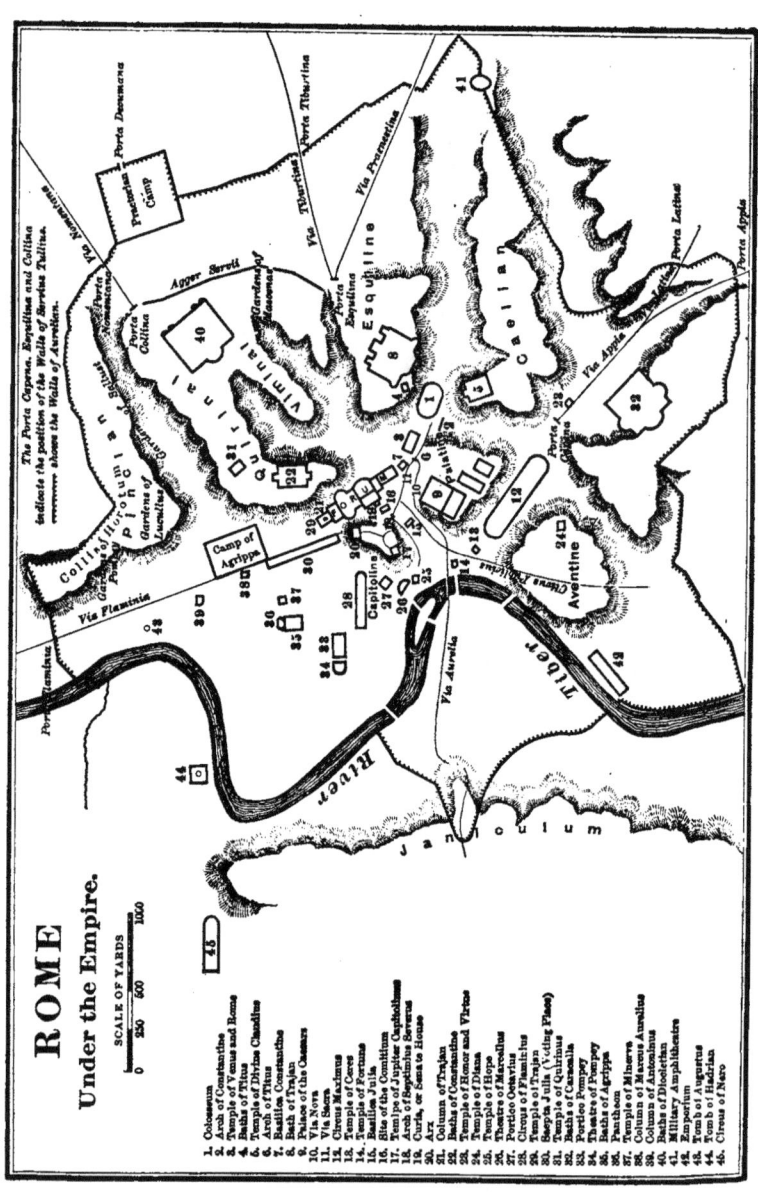

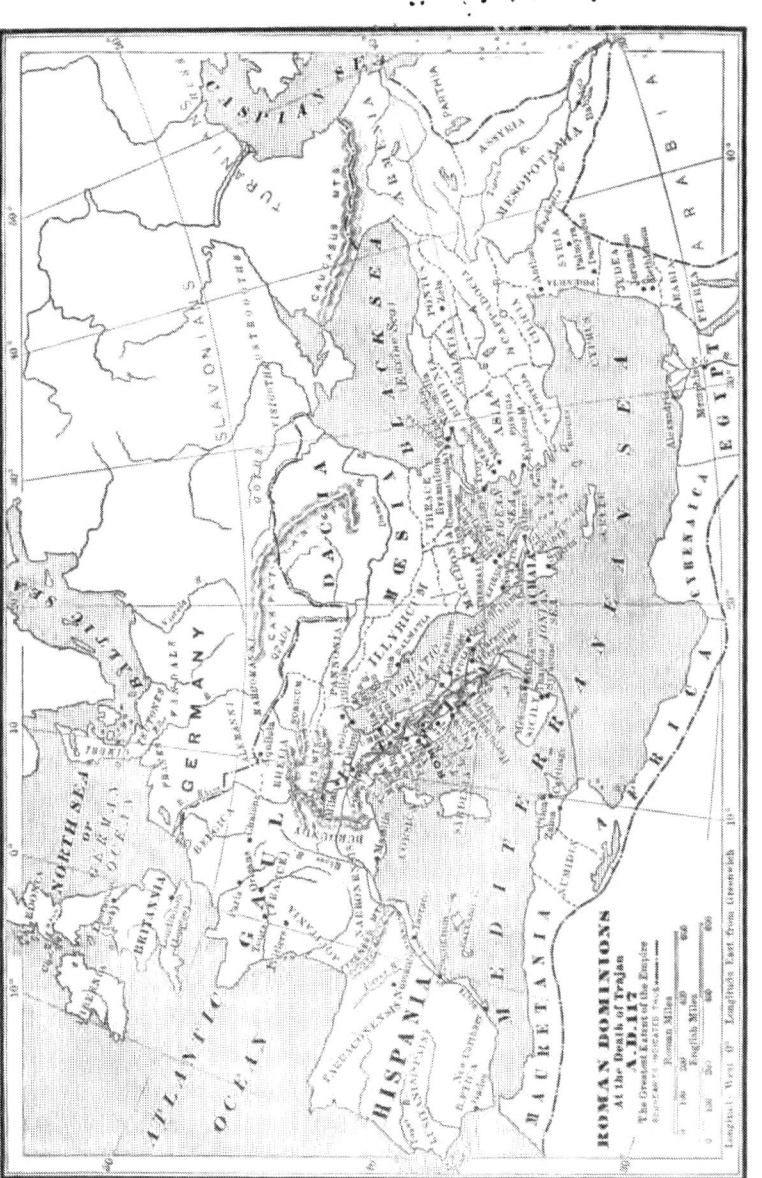

THE FIRST PERIOD
ROME AS A KINGDOM

I

THE LEGENDS OF THE SEVEN KINGS OF ROME

IN Troy, a famous town of Asia Minor, there once lived a man named Æ-ne′as. For ten long years the Greeks, fierce enemies of the Trojans, had been trying to take the city; and at length they succeeded. They set fire to it, and soon the whole town was in flames. Æneas fought as long as there was any hope in fighting, then he took his aged father on his shoulders, and keeping fast hold of the hand of his little son As-ca′ni-us, he fled through the burning streets and over the ruins of the walls to the country. Many of his friends joined him, and they hid away together among the mountains. After a while the gods told Æneas to build some boats and set out on the sea, for he

FLIGHT OF ÆNEAS
(From a Painting in the Vatican at Rome)
Raphael

and his companions must make a new home for themselves in Italy.

They obeyed and set sail, and after many troubles and adventures they reached the Italian shores. Æneas married La-vin'i-a, the daughter of the king of La'ti-um,[1] and afterward became ruler of that province. He built a town which he named La-vin'i-um, in honor of his wife. After he died, Ascanius ruled; but he soon found that his town was becoming too crowded. He concluded, therefore, to leave it and build another on a ridge of a neighboring hill. This he named Al'ba Lon'ga, or the long white city.

For three hundred years the descendants of Ascanius ruled in Latium. Then there was trouble. The rightful king was Nu'mi-tor, but his brother A-mu'li-us stole the kingdom and murdered Numitor's son. There was also a daughter, Rhe'a Syl'vi-a, but Amulius disposed of her by making her a priestess of the goddess Ves'ta. One day Amulius was told that his niece had twin sons whose father was the war god Mars. "If they are allowed to live, they will grow up and claim the kingdom," thought Amulius; so he put Rhea Sylvia to death and ordered one of his men to throw the boys into the river Ti'ber. The man obeyed, but the river had overflowed its banks, and when it went down again, it left the two babies on dry land at the foot of the Pal'a-tine Hill, not drowned by any means, but exceedingly hungry and crying with all their might. A she wolf coming for a drink heard the crying and went to the children. She seemed to think they were some

---

[1] Pronounce La'shi-um. Note that *c*, *s*, and *t*, preceded by an accented vowel and followed by *i* with another vowel, take the sound of *sh*.

LEGENDS OF THE SEVEN KINGS OF ROME

new kind of cub, for she carried them to her den and nursed them there for some time. At length they were discovered by a shepherd named Faus'tu-lus. He frightened the wolf away and carried the babies home to his wife. When Rom'-u-lus and Re'mus, as they were called, had grown up, Faustulus told them that they were not his children, but the grandsons of Numitor, and that Numitor was the rightful king. Then the young men and their shepherd friends overcame the wicked Amulius. He was put to death, and the kingdom was given back to Numitor.

THE FINDING OF ROMULUS AND REMUS

The two brothers determined to form a kingdom for themselves, and to build a city near the place where they had been thrown into the water. But now there was trouble, for it was fitting that the elder brother should give his name to the city, and they were twins! "Let the gods decide," they said. So Romulus climbed the Palatine Hill and Remus the Av'en-tine, and they watched all day and all night; but the gods gave them no sign. Just at sunrise, however, Remus saw six vultures fly across the sky. His followers shouted with delight and hailed him as king. While they were still shouting, the friends of Romulus cried out joyfully; for, behold, Romulus had seen a flight of twelve vultures! But who could say whether it was worth more to see six birds first or twelve birds second?

The question seems to have been settled in some way in favor of Romulus, for he began to build on the Palatine Hill a wall for a town. Remus jumped over it and said scornfully, "That is what your enemies will do." "And this is the way they will fare," retorted Romulus, and struck his brother angrily. Remus fell down dead, and all his life Romulus grieved for the brother whom he had slain in a moment of anger.

The walls were completed and the place was named Rome; but it needed people. "I will admit as citizens whoever choose to come," said Romulus; and at this, there came crowds of men who had fled from their enemies or from justice. Romulus took them in and protected them.

Rome became strong, but the men of the neighboring states looked upon it scornfully and would not allow their daughters to marry Romans. "If you want wives to match your men," they said to Romulus, "you would better open an asylum for women slaves and thieves and outcasts."

Romulus kept his temper, and a little later he even invited his scornful neighbors to some games in honor of Nep'tune. All were curious to see the new city, and they did not wait for any urging. The Sa'bines especially came in full numbers and brought their wives and children also. The Romans entertained them hospitably, and soon the guests were all eagerly watching the games. Suddenly the Romans rushed upon their visitors, seized the young maidens among them, and carried them away to become their wives.

LEGENDS OF THE SEVEN KINGS OF ROME 5

Then the Romans fought with one tribe after another, — with the Sabines last of all, because these people waited till they were fully prepared to fight. The most important thing for the Sabines to do was to take the Roman citadel, that is, the strong fortress which Romulus had built on a hill to protect the city, and they secretly asked the young girl Tar-pe′i-a,[1] daughter of the Roman commander, what reward she would demand to let them in. "Give me what you wear on your left arms," she replied, pointing to their heavy golden bracelets. They agreed and she opened the gate. But they also carried their shields upon their left arms, and they felt such scorn for the disloyal maiden that they threw these upon her, and so crushed her to death. That is why the cliff on one side of the ledge on which the citadel stood is called the Tarpeian Rock. For many years afterward, traitors were punished by being hurled from this very cliff.

When the Sabines were once within the city, a savage fight followed between them and the Romans; but now the stolen women had a word to say. Their husbands had treated them kindly and they had become fond of their new homes. They ran fearlessly into the battle, straight between the angry fighters, and begged on the one side their fathers, and on the other their husbands, not to murder one another. The men were so amazed that they stopped fighting, and after a parley they agreed to make peace and even to dwell together as one nation.

Many of the ideas and customs of Rome, which were

[1] Pronounce Tar-pe′ya. Note that *i* preceded by an accented vowel, and followed by an unaccented one, has the sound of *y* in *yes*.

SABINE WOMEN STOPPING THE FIGHT
(From a Painting in the Louvre, Paris)

handed down from the time of Romulus, were quite different from those of to-day. For instance, the father of a family owned his wife and children as much as he owned his sword or his house, and he could do what he liked with them. If he wished to sell them as slaves, or even to put them to death, there was no law to prevent.

A group of families claiming to be the descendants of a common ancestor was known as a *gens*, or *clan*. The head of each gens was called a *pater*, the Latin word for *father*, and therefore the members of these early clans came to be known as pa-tri'cians. They were the aristocrats of Rome. All the patricians were divided into three large groups called *tribes*, each tribe consisting of ten smaller groups called *cú'ri-æ*.

Besides these patricians there were slaves and clients. The slaves were few in number and were chiefly house servants. The clients were for the most part strangers who had come to Rome, or else freedmen, that is, slaves who had become free. They depended upon some patrician to act as their patron, that is, to befriend them in whatever way a man of power and standing could aid one of lower rank. In return, they acted as humble friends to him. If they were poor, they worked on his land; if they became rich, they made him generous gifts. The patricians were not all wealthy by any means, and to make money in trade seemed to them a disgrace. Through their clients, however, they could carry on trade without humiliating themselves.

Besides patricians, slaves, and clients, there was a great multitude of people in Rome who were known as ple-be'ians, from *plebs*, a Latin word meaning *common folk*. They were people, or the descendants of people, who had come to Rome later than the patrician families. Some were freedmen, some had fled to the city for refuge, and some had probably been conquered in war. They were not forbidden to carry on trade, but most of them worked on the land.

The patricians had many rights which the plebeians did not share. The patrician alone might marry into a patrician family, or leave his property by will to whomever he chose. No plebeian was allowed these rights. The patrician was the only voter, and he alone was allowed to hold office. Neither slaves, clients, nor plebeians were regarded as citizens. The patrician was the only citizen.

The government of Rome was carried on by the king, the senate, and the citizens. The king acted as priest, ruler, and commander; that is, he was the religious head of the Romans, he governed them in time of peace, and he led them to battle in time of war. He had a right to name his successor. The senate was composed of elderly men selected from the heads of the patrician families. It took its name from the Latin word *senex*, meaning an *old man*. No resolution could become law without its approval. The senate also acted as special adviser to the king; and if he died without naming a successor, it had power to nominate a sovereign. The citizens, — that is, the patricians, — took part in the government by voting in the assembly of the curiæ known as the *co-mi'ti-a cu-ri-a'ta*. Each of the thirty curiæ had one vote. Laws might be proposed in this assembly either by the assembly itself or by the king, but, as has been said, they must be approved by the senate. No king, whether named by the preceding ruler or nominated by the senate, could take possession of the throne until the comitia curiata had given its consent.

These were some of the customs that are said to have flourished in early Rome. The little village grew in power and in number of inhabitants until Romulus had become an old man. When the time had drawn near for him to be taken to the gods, he called his people to a sacred festival. A terrible thunderstorm arose, and it became so dark that they could not see one another's faces. When the light had come again, the royal seat was vacant; Romulus had vanished. His people mourned for him, but after a while a man who was held in much esteem among them declared that their lost ruler had appeared to him in a vision as one of the gods. "The king bade me tell you," said the man, "that the gods decree Rome to become the capital of the world, and that if you cultivate the art of war, no human power will be able to withstand you. Then he vanished into the heavens." The Romans believed the story, and after this they worshiped Romulus as a god.

This is the legend of the founding of Rome. The Roman poets and orators were never tired of referring to it, and in the magnificent temple of Ju'pi-ter, called the Capitol, which in later days stood on the Tarpeian Rock, there was a large statue of the wolf and the twin brothers.

SUMMARY

After the fall of Troy, Æneas went to Italy and founded Lavinium. His son Ascanius founded Alba Longa.

Amulius stole the kingdom from his brother Numitor, and made Rhea Silvia a Vestal virgin. She became the mother of Romulus and Remus. The boys were thrown into the Tiber, but were nursed by a wolf and brought up by Faustulus. When they were grown up, they restored the kingdom to Numitor. Romulus founded Rome in 753 (?) B. C., having slain his brother in a moment of anger. He admitted as citizens all who chose to come. To obtain wives for them, he stole the women of the Sabines and others. War followed. By the disloyalty of Tarpeia, the Sabines were permitted to enter the city. The stolen women made peace between the two nations.

The people of Rome were divided into patricians, clients, slaves, and plebeians. The patrician alone had the rights of a citizen. The government was carried on by the king, the senate, and the citizens. The senate was made up of the heads of families. The assembly of patricians, or citizens, was called the comitia curiata.

After Romulus had been taken to the gods, he appeared in a vision and predicted that Rome would become the capital of the world.

SUGGESTIONS FOR WRITTEN WORK

Ascanius describes his flight from Troy.
The story that Faustulus told Romulus and Remus.
The Sabine women plan together to make peace.
A Roman boy describes the disappearance of Romulus.

II

THE LEGENDS OF THE SEVEN KINGS OF ROME
(Continued)

BESIDES the story of Romulus and Remus, the Romans had many other legends about the early days of their city. According to these legends, Romulus was the first of seven kings. It took a whole year to choose his successor, for the Romans wanted a Roman and the Sabines wanted a Sabine. At length they came to an exceedingly wise agreement; the Romans were to choose the king, but he was to be of the Sabine race. They chose a wise, just man named Nu′ma Pom-pil′i-us. He saw that his subjects were brave, but that they were a rude, savage people who needed to be taught everything except how to fight.

First of all, he made treaties with the tribes around, in order that there might be a time of peace. Then he set to work to instruct his people how to worship the gods. They believed that the goddess E-ge'ri-a used to come to him in a certain shady grove and tell him what to teach them, and therefore they paid close attention to his words.

He appointed priests to carry on the worship of Jupiter, Mars, and some of the other gods, and gave them salaries and handsome robes. The priests of Mars wore richly embroidered tunics and carried shields. They used to march through the city in procession, singing hymns to the war-god and carrying on a solemn dance.

MARS
(In the Ludovisi Villa at Rome)

Numa had it carefully written out in just what manner the worship of each god was to be carried on, what sacrifices were to be offered, and in what manner. He gave the charge of this worship to the *pon'ti-fex max'i-mus*,[1] or high priest, and taught him also how to tell the will of the gods from flashes of lightning and the flight of birds.

Thus far, the Romans had been busy chiefly with fighting, but Numa divided among them the lands which Romulus had won, and encouraged them to cultivate the ground. He marked out their fields with stones; and to make them feel it a crime to remove these stones, he set up an altar on the Cap'i-to-line Hill in honor of Ter'mi-nus, the god of boundaries. He also built a temple in honor of Ja'nus. In time of war its doors were open, but in peace they were closed; and it is the greatest glory of the reign of Numa that while he was on the throne the gates were always closed.

ETRUSCAN WARRIOR
(From a Bronze Statuette)

The gates of this temple were flung open, however, almost as soon as Numa died, and a new king, Tul'lus Hos-til'i-us, was chosen. He believed that his people would become slow and dull if they gave up fighting, and therefore he seized the first excuse for a war, and in a little while the Romans and the people of Alba Longa were drawn up on the field of battle. While both lines were awaiting the signal to make an attack, the Alban general asked to speak with

[1] See picture on page 170.

LEGENDS OF THE SEVEN KINGS OF ROME 13

King Tullus. "The E-trus'cans who dwell all about us," he said, "are a very powerful people both by land and by sea. Now when we and you are exhausted by fighting, they may fall upon us and destroy both parties. Can we not come to terms in some other way than by war?"

Tullus would have much preferred to fight, but he could not help seeing that this was a sensible speech, and after a while a plan was made that must have disappointed the Etruscans if they had been hoping to get any gain from the quarrel. It chanced that in the Roman army were three brothers of the Ho-ra'tian family born at one birth. They were known as the Ho-ra'ti-i. In the Alban army were their three cousins, also born at one birth, of the Cu-ri-a'tian family. They were known as the Cu-ri-a'ti-i. The leaders of the armies agreed that these six should meet in combat, three on a side, and the nation whose champions won should be looked upon as the victors. "Be brave," cried both parties to their respective champions. "Remember that your gods, your country, your parents, that all your countrymen, both here and at home, are watching you." The champions took their stand between

Lebarbier
CONTEST BETWEEN THE HORATII AND CURIATII

the two lines. The signal was given, and in a moment their swords were flashing. The encounter was so fierce that almost at once two of the Horatii fell dead and the three Curiatii were wounded. Hurt as they were, they were together more than a match for the remaining one of the Horatii; but he had no idea of allowing all three to attack him at once. He ran away and they pursued. He who was least wounded came up to Ho-ra'ti-us first. The Roman suddenly turned upon him and slew him. He did the same with the other two as they came up; and so it was that the Romans became the victors.

The Roman army shouted for joy, and soon set out upon the return home. First came men bearing the armor and weapons of the Curiatii. Next came Horatius, and after him the rest of the army. When they reached the city gates, the people poured out to welcome them; but the sister of Horatius gave a great wail of sorrow, for on her brother's shoulders she recognized the coat of one of the Curiatii to whom she had been betrothed, a coat which she herself had wrought. Horatius drew his sword and ran it through her body, crying, "So perish every Roman woman who shall mourn an enemy." Every one was dismayed. The murder of the maiden must be punished, but how could they put to death the man who had just saved them from being subject to the Albans? Finally Horatius was brought to trial. His father pleaded so earnestly for his son's life that the champion was pardoned; but many sacrifices were offered to the gods that his sin might be forgiven.

The Albans were not very faithful subjects, and at length

Tullus commanded them to remove to Rome. He sent soldiers to tear down their homes, and with pitiful weeping and wailing, the poor people caught up whatever they valued most of their household treasures and went in sorrowful groups to Rome. The temples of the gods were left standing, but everything else in Alba Longa was destroyed.

Tullus fought other wars, and was so successful that he began to feel it quite beneath so great a man as he to pay any service to the gods or even to deal justly and lawfully with his people. The gods were angry, and they sent a pestilence upon people and king. Then Tullus was ready enough to offer up sacrifices. Unluckily for him, he had neglected this duty for so long that he did not know how to observe the rites properly. Jupiter was angry, and with a flash of lightning he burned the king and his house to ashes.

OFFERING UP A SACRIFICE

The next king was An'cus Mar'ti-us. He was a grandson of Numa Pompilius; and he seemed to have the good traits of both Numa and Tullus. First of all, he had the rules for the proper worship of the gods carefully written on tablets and set out where every one could read them. He paid such attention to his religious duties that the neighboring nations thought there was an excellent chance for them to attack the city while the Roman king was saying prayers and offering up sacrifices. They made a mistake, for King Ancus could fight as well as pray. He conquered his enemies and strengthened the fortifications of Rome. Just across the river Tiber was the hill Ja-nic'u-lum, and Ancus did not forget to fortify this, lest some enemy should capture it and so be able to take the town. In order to join this hill to the city, he built a wooden bridge across the Tiber, and at the mouth of the river he founded a colony which he called Os'ti-a, the Latin name for *mouths*.

King Ancus committed only one act that seemed foolish: when he came to die, he made one Lu'ci-us Tar-quin'i-us Pris'cus guardian of his two sons. This man was rich and ambitious, and he had come to Rome on purpose to win power. When he was on his way to the city for the first time, with his wife Tan'a-quil beside him in the chariot, and had come as far as the hill Janiculum, an eagle suddenly swooped down, caught his hat from his head and wheeled about in the air with it, then dropped down and placed it on his head again. Tanaquil was skilled in reading the flights of birds and other omens, and she cried out with delight, "The eagle is the bird of Jupiter, and most surely some lofty station in life is awaiting you." Tarquinius bought a house in Rome and tried by every means in his power to win the favor of the king and the chief men, and he was most successful.

Now when Ancus was dead and the people were about to choose a new ruler, Tarquinius Priscus sent the two sons of Ancus away on a hunting trip, and then he made a speech to the assembly, telling them why they would do well to make him king. He seems to have convinced them, for he was chosen sovereign. No one could say that he did not do well by his kingdom, for he conquered the tribes roundabout, and even the powerful Etruscans acknowledged him as their king, and sent him a crown and sceptre and ivory chair, an embroidered tunic, a purple toga, or robe, and twelve bundles of rods called *fasces*, in each of which was an axe. This last was to signify that he had power to punish and to put to death. The men who carried the rods and axes were known as *lictors;* and when the king appeared in public, twelve of them always marched in single file before him.

After the enemies of the Romans had been subdued, Tarquinius set to work to improve the city. In honor of Jupiter, he built a splendid temple which was called the Capitol. The height on which it stood received the name of the Capitoline Hill. He also built directly across the city a famous underground sewer called the Clo-a'ca Max'i-ma, or *great sewer*, to drain the swamps between the hills, and he marked out the Circus Maximus, or *great circus*, where games were held.

LICTOR

One night the king and queen were aroused from their sleep to see a wonderful sight. A little boy, the son of one of their slaves, lay fast asleep, and around his head was blazing a beautiful and harmless flame. Queen Tanaquil forbade the servants to disturb the child, and she said to her husband, "Of course that fire is a mark of the favor of the gods, and the boy is surely destined for some noble position. Let us bring him up with the best of care, and if ever we are in the darkness of adversity, he will be a light to us." From that time Tarquinius treated the boy as his own son, and when

CLOACA MAXIMA

he was grown up, he showed himself so truly kingly that the king gave him his daughter in marriage.

The sons of Ancus seem to have been waiting patiently, expecting that the crown would be theirs at the death of Tarquinius; but when they saw that the king's favor was given to the boy Ser'vi-us Tul'li-us, they were angry and indignant, and a little later they hired two bold and daring shepherds to assassinate Tarquinius. Probably the sons of Ancus would have been able to seize the crown if Queen Tanaquil had not been so quick-witted. She opened the window and addressed the people. "Be of good cheer," she said. "The king is only stunned, and I hope you will soon see him again. In the mean time, he wishes you to obey Servius Tullius in his place." Then to Servius she said, "Now is your time. If you are a man, the kingdom is yours, not theirs who have brought about the murder of the king." Servius seated

LEGENDS OF THE SEVEN KINGS OF ROME

himself upon the throne and gave judgment in some cases, while in others he pretended to consult the king. By the time that the king's death was known, Servius had gained so much power that he easily held the kingdom. He was just and kind to his people. He never forgot that his mother had been a slave, and he was so strong a friend to the poorer folk that it is no wonder they called him the good king Servius.

In some ways the reign of Servius Tullius was almost a revolution. First of all, he planned for a larger army. It had always been regarded as an honor to defend the state, and therefore only patricians had been privileged to serve as soldiers. Servius, however, obliged all landowners to join the army. He divided them, not into patricians and plebeians, but into five classes according to the amount of land which they held. The largest landowners were required to provide themselves with horses to form the cavalry; the next largest had to obtain full suits of armor, helmets, coats of mail, shields, and greaves, or protectors for the legs. The poorer people provided less armor. The patricians as a class were more wealthy than the plebeians; in general, therefore, the former continued to serve as cavalry, while the latter made up the infantry.

ROMAN SOLDIER WITH SCALE ARMOR

To make it easier to form the army, Servius paid no attention to the old division of the patricians into three tribes;

instead, he divided the city into four wards, or districts, classing all landowners living in one district, whether patricians or plebeians, as of one tribe.

Servius built a wall entirely around the city, parts of which remain to this day. He also established the census, a list of the people of the state, their children, and the amount of their property. This census was taken every five years. It closed with a sacrifice to the gods called a *lustrum*, or *purification*, and soon the period of five years came to be called a lustrum.

The place where the soldiers used to come together to drill was a plain just outside the walls of the city called the Campus Martius, or Field of Mars. The troops were divided into groups of one hundred, and as the Latin word for *hundred* is *centum*, the meeting of these groups came to be called the *comitia cen-tu-ri-a'ta*, or *assembly of the centuries*.

TULLIA DRIVING OVER THE BODY OF HER FATHER

Servius was loved by his people, but there was one man whom he feared, Lucius, the son of Tarquinius. Lucius had married the daughter of Servius; but she was a wicked woman and plotted that her husband should seize her father's crown. One day Lucius went in royal robes to the forum, or public square, and declared that he, and not the son of a slave, was the rightful king. He caught hold of the aged Servius and flung him down the steps of the senate house, and then sent men to murder him. The wicked daughter of Servius heard what had been done, and she hastened to the forum to salute her husband as king. He bade her withdraw from such a tumult, and she obeyed, ordering her charioteer to drive her chariot over the bleeding body of her father lying in the road.

So it was that a second Lucius Tarquinius became king. He was so cruel and haughty that the people called him Tarquinius Su-per′bus, or Tarquin *the Proud*, and if he had not always kept a bodyguard around him, some one would surely have murdered him. One day when he was at the height of his power, a strange woman came before him with nine books, and asked him to buy them. Her price was so high that he only laughed scornfully. She went away and burned three of the books, then returned

MOUNTED OFFICER
(From a Statue in Naples)

and offered him the six at the same price that she had asked for the nine. "The woman is surely mad," Tarquinius declared. She made no reply, but went away again, and a little later offered him the last three books, but still at the same price. The affair was so remarkable that Tarquinius began to think the books must have been sent by the gods. He paid the price and took them. They proved to be prophecies about the future of the city. They were preserved with the utmost care and were consulted whenever the city seemed to be in danger. The strange woman was the Sib'yl of Cu'mæ. She vanished and was never seen again. The books were known as the Sib'yl-line Books, and were counted among the greatest treasures of Rome.

Tarquinius was successful in war, but he could not subdue the Ga'bi-i. This his false son Sex'tus undertook to do for him. He fled to them covered with blood and begged them to protect him from his father. They treated him kindly, and gave him command of a band of soldiers. In the first engagement, Sextus and his band put the Romans to flight — for this was what he and Tarquinius had agreed upon. Now the Gabii were so sure that Sextus was true to them that they made him leader of their whole army. Then Sextus treacherously surrendered the town to the Romans.

Tarquinius had done so many evil deeds that it is small wonder he became afraid the gods would punish him. A serpent gliding out of a wooden pillar frightened him, and he sent two of his sons to the oracle of the Greeks at Del'phi to ask what the sight foreboded. With them went their cousin, who was called Bru'tus, or *the fool*, because he pre-

LEGENDS OF THE SEVEN KINGS OF ROME

tended to be foolish lest Tarquinius should put him to death. The two sons had a question of their own to ask: Who would reign after their father? The oracle replied, "He who first kisses his mother." When they returned to Rome, Brutus pretended to stumble and fell. No one noticed that he slyly kissed the ground, and no one knew until afterwards that he said to himself, "The earth is the mother of us all."

Sextus, who had deceived the Gabii, was the worst of the three sons. One day he insulted so grievously the good Lu-cre'-ti-a, wife of one of his cousins, that she called upon her father and her husband to avenge her, and then in grief and shame she plunged a knife into her heart. At this Brutus stood out boldly before the people and recounted the evil deeds of Tarquinius and his sons. He pleaded with the Romans to drive the tyrant from the throne, and they agreed. Moreover, they declared that never again should a king reign over them, and they even decreed that if any one should venture to say he wished a return of the kingly rule, he should be put to death as an enemy to the state. This took place in 509 B.C. That date marks the end of the kingdom, for Rome now became a republic.

ARMY-LEADER IN HIS MANTLE

SUMMARY

The six kings who followed Romulus were: —

1. Numa Pompilius, who taught his people to worship the gods and cultivate the ground.

2. Tullus Hostilius, who became ruler of Alba Longa by the victory of Horatius over the Curiatii.

3. Ancus Martius, who attended closely to his religious duties and strengthened the fortifications of Rome.

4. Lucius Tarquinius Priscus, who overcame the Etruscans, and built the Capitol, the Cloaca Maxima, and the Circus Maximus.

5. Servius Tullius, who required all landowners to join the army, and divided the people into five classes according to their property in land. He divided the city into four wards, he built a wall around it, and established the census. The comitia centuriata originated in his reign.

6. Tarquinius Superbus, who murdered Servius Tullius. He purchased the Sibylline Books. His son Sextus overcame the Gabii by treachery. Brutus aroused the Romans to expel the king. The kingdom now became a republic.

SUGGESTIONS FOR WRITTEN WORK

An Alban woman tells the story of her removal to Rome.
Describe the Capitol (from a picture).
Tanaquil tells Servius of the "harmless flame."
The coming of the Sibyl as described by Tarquinius.

THE SECOND PERIOD

ROME AS A REPUBLIC

I

THE ATTEMPTS OF TARQUINIUS TO REGAIN HIS KINGDOM

THE Romans had refused to be under a king, and they were afraid that if any one man were made chief ruler, he would become too powerful. They decided, therefore, to elect two rulers instead of one, and for a term of one year only. These two were called *consuls*. They wore robes with borders of deep violet and sat in seats of honor known as curule chairs. These chairs were either made of ivory or richly ornamented with it, but, however handsome and honorable they may have been, they must have seemed rather uncomfortable, for they had neither arms nor back. According to law, neither consul could give a command if the other objected. This was all very well when matters were going on smoothly, but in time of danger, if an enemy were at the gate, for instance, the two consuls might have quite different schemes for defense, and while they were trying to convince each other, the enemy might force his way into the city. The Romans were too keen not to provide for this, and they decreed that if great public danger arose, a dictator should be appointed. He was to hold power for six months only, but during that time even the consuls were to obey his commands.

Brutus was one of the first consuls; but it was not long before he must have wished he was only a private citizen, for his two sons were brought before him to be punished. They

BRUTUS CONDEMNING HIS SONS TO DEATH
(From a Painting in the Louvre)

had conspired to bring back King Tarquinius. Brutus must have been heartbroken, but he gave sentence according to law, and sat by sternly while his own sons, together with the other conspirators, were flogged and then beheaded.

Tarquinius still hoped to regain his crown, and he induced one tribe after another to take up his cause and fight for him. In one of the battles Brutus was slain. His fellow consul,

Pub'li-us Va-le'ri-us, was now left sole ruler; and the people began to be afraid that he would try to make himself king. It was dangerous even to be suspected of such a desire, and he did all in his power to show that he never thought of such a thing. He built his house at the foot of a hill instead of on top, as he had begun; he had the axes removed from the bundles of rods that were borne before him by the lictors; and, far more important than these acts, he had a law passed that a Roman citizen who was sentenced by any one except a dictator to be put to death, or to be flogged, might appeal to the assembly of the centuries. This was named the Va-le'ri-an Law.

Tarquinius had not given up hope of the throne, and now he persuaded Lars Por'se-na of Clu'si-um to become his ally. Then there was dismay in Rome, for Porsena was a powerful king and could call out many thousands of men. His great army came marching toward the city. From the Tarpeian Rock, men could see one little village after another burst into flames. The countryfolk seized whatever was

THE CLIFFS OF THE CAPITOLINE HILL
(Known as the Tarpeian Rock)

dearest to them and fled to the protection of the city walls. Lars Porsena came nearer; he captured Janiculum; and so great was the alarm of the Roman soldiers that they ran headlong across the bridge and into the town, as frightened as the women and children of the country.

> Out spake the Consul roundly:
> "The bridge must straight go down,
> For, since Janiculum is lost,
> Naught else can save the town."[1]

Then a brave Roman named Horatius stepped forward and spoke to the Consul:

> "Hew down the bridge, Sir Consul,
> With all the speed ye may;
> I, with two more to help me,
> Will hold the foe in play.
> In yon strait path a thousand
> May well be stopped by three.
> Now who will stand on either hand,
> And keep the bridge with me?"
>
> Then out spake Spu′ri-us Lar′ti-us;
> A Ram′ni-an proud was he:
> "Lo, I will stand at thy right hand,
> And keep the bridge with thee."
> And out spake strong Her-min′i-us;
> Of Tit′i-an blood was he:
> "I will abide on thy left side,
> And keep the bridge with thee."

Soon Porsena and his followers were shouting with laughter to see "the dauntless three" take their stand to drive back an army. There was terrible fighting; but all the while

[1] *Horatius*, by T. B. Macaulay.

the Romans, — consul, fathers, and plebeians, were breaking down the bridge. It was ready to crumble.

"Come back, come back, Horatius!"
Loud cried the Fathers all.
"Back, Lartius! back, Herminius!
Back, ere the ruin fall!"

Lartius and Herminius darted back over the swaying timbers, and Horatius stood alone on the farther shore between the

HORATIUS KEEPING THE BRIDGE

river and his sixty thousand foes. Then he sprang into the flood, wounded, and weighed down by his armor as he was.

And when above the surges
They saw his crest appear,
All Rome sent forth a rapturous cry,
And even the ranks of Tus'ca-ny
Could scarce forbear to cheer.

He swam bravely to the landing-place; he had saved his country.

> And wives still pray to Ju'no
> For boys with hearts as bold
> As his who kept the bridge so well
> In the brave days of old.

Even after this, there was sore trouble in Rome, for Lars Porsena besieged the town and famine set in. Then Ca'i-us Mu'ci-us, a noble young Roman, made his way into the enemy's camp to kill the king. By mistake, he slew, not the king, but his secretary. When he was brought before Lars Porsena, he was threatened with being burned alive if he did not reveal whatever plots had been made. He stretched forth his right hand and held it in the fire that was burning on the altar. "See," he said to the king, "how little those think of the body who have glory in view." Lars Porsena was too brave a man not to appreciate bravery, and he ordered the young man to be sent home unharmed. Mucius told him that three hundred other youths were sworn to have his life; and Lars Porsena soon asked the Romans to make a treaty of peace with him. Caius Mucius was richly rewarded by his countrymen, and the name

MUCIUS HOLDING HIS HAND IN THE FIRE

THE ATTEMPTS OF TARQUINIUS

Scæv'o-la, or *the left-handed*, was given him in memory of his deed.

Tarquinius now induced the powerful Latins to help him. At Lake Re-gil'lus there was a fierce battle between the Romans on one side and the Latins and Etruscans on the other. The Romans were getting the worst of it when suddenly the twin gods, Cas'tor and Pol'lux, appeared among them. The armor of the gods and also their steeds were white as snow, and they had come to the aid of the Romans.

> And forthwith all the ranks of Rome
> Were bold and of good cheer;

and soon the battle was won. Tarquinius Superbus gave no further trouble, and Rome never had another king.

SUMMARY

Instead of one king, two consuls were elected; but in great public danger supreme command was to be given to a dictator. During the consulship of Brutus, his two sons were beheaded as traitors. Brutus's colleague Valerius had the Valerian Law passed, giving to citizens condemned to death or to be flogged, the right of appeal to the assembly of the centuries.

Lars Porsena became an ally of Tarquinius. Rome was saved by the bravery of Horatius. Porsena, moved by the courage of Scævola, made peace with the Romans.

The Latins now aided Tarquinius. Castor and Pollux came to the help of the Romans at Lake Regillus. Tarquinius made no further trouble.

SUGGESTIONS FOR WRITTEN WORK

Why was it better to have two consuls than one king?
Valerius tells why he wishes the Valerian Law to be passed.
Lars Porsena tells his little son the story of Horatius at the bridge.

IV

HOW THE PLEBEIANS WON THEIR RIGHTS

THE preceding stories of gods and kings and heroes are told of the first two hundred and fifty years after the supposed date of the founding of Rome, that is, from 753 B. C. to 496 B. C. In one way they are false. For instance, there never was a god Mars to be the father of Romulus and Remus; and no nation ever suddenly gave up fighting and began to spend the time in cultivating the ground, as the legends say was done in the days of Numa. Indeed, there is no authentic history of Rome with definite dates until at earliest 390 B. C. Nevertheless, even in the most impossible of these stories there is always some bit of truth for a foundation. By searching for this, we learn that Rome was founded by the Latins to protect them from the Etruscans; that after much hard fighting, two other villages united with the Romans, took the level space between the two hills for their forum, or public square, and built on the Capitoline Hill a strong citadel, or fort, which should serve to defend them both; and that later they were joined by other settlers who lived on the Cæ′li-an Hill. Rome is said to have been founded 753 B. C. A century

HOW THE PLEBEIANS WON THEIR RIGHTS 33

and a half later, the city walls, then nearly five miles in length, inclosed seven hills, the Qui-ri'nal, Vim'i-nal, Es'-

RUINS OF THE ROMAN FORUM

qui-line, Cælian, Aventine, Palatine, and Capitoline. That is why Rome is often spoken of as the seven-hilled city.

The chief reason why Rome grew so rapidly was because it had so excellent a location. There were other groups of hills in Italy and other settlements on them, but in these other groups, the hills were higher and farther apart, and the settlements could be independent of one another and did not have to unite; therefore they increased in size slowly. In another way the location of Rome was most desirable. It was beside the Tiber, and for that reason the Romans could carry on trade with all the districts through which the Tiber and its branches flowed. Moreover, it was far enough from the sea to be safe from the attacks of pirates. No other town in Italy had so many advantages.

There was one great disadvantage, however, and this was that the people were not united. Servius Tullius had done a good deal to bring them together when he admitted all landowners to the army, but the old distinction of patricians and plebeians was by no means forgotten, and the patricians still had many privileges which were not shared by the plebeians.

In all the fighting between the Romans and the friends of Tarquinius, the plebeians had suffered most. When there was warfare in the summer, most of the patricians could have their land cared for by slaves; but the plebeian had to go to the army and leave his farm with no one to cultivate it or gather in the crops. He was fortunate if the enemy did not destroy the crops altogether, steal the cattle, and burn the house. The plebeian was required to pay taxes, but he received no pay for his service in the army, and no one thought of asking the state to make good his losses. The result was that the plebeian must either starve or borrow of some patrician.

Borrowing was dangerous business in Rome. If a man did not pay his debt within thirty days of the appointed time, the law was that he should be imprisoned, loaded down with chains, and fed on bread and water for thirty days. If he did not pay then, he might be sold as a slave or even put to death. One day, fifteen years after Tarquinius was driven out, an old man came into the forum. His clothes were nothing but rags, and he was thin and pale. The people gathered around him. "I know him," said more than one of them. "He was an officer and a brave soldier. See on

HOW THE PLEBEIANS WON THEIR RIGHTS

his breast the scars of his wounds." The old man told them his pitiful story. "While I was in the army," he said, "the enemy destroyed my crops, drove away my cattle, and burned my house. I had to pay a tax, and the only thing to do was to borrow money. I could not repay it, and my creditor beat me. Behold!" He threw off his robe from his shoulders, and the crowd saw the bloody marks of the whip. The plebeians were furious. "Call the senate together," they demanded, "and make laws that are just to us." The senators were so frightened that they did not know whether there was more danger in staying at home or going to the senate house, but at length they came together and began to discuss what should be done. Suddenly some Latin horsemen galloped up to the city. "The enemy is at hand!" they cried. "Call out the army." But the plebeians would not be called out. "Why should we fight for Rome?" they demanded, "when warfare brings us nothing but debt and ruin? Let those fight who gain by war." One of the consuls promised that if they would join the army, he would propose a just law for debtors. The plebeians trusted him, and the enemy was

ROMAN SOLDIER

driven away; but the other consul, Ap'pi-us Clau'di-us, led the senate to refuse to make any change in the laws. Then the plebeians were angry indeed. "Why should we stay in Rome?" they said to one another. "Why not leave the city and found a city of our own?" They decided to do this, and one day they set out for a hill a few miles away and made ready to build themselves houses.

Then the patricians were disturbed, for they had lost the cultivators of the ground. "Let them go," said Appius Claudius scornfully; "we have no need of the rabble." Fortunately, the other chief men were wiser, and it was decided to send three patricians to try to persuade them to return. But they would not be persuaded. Then Me-ne'ni-us A-grip'pa told them a little story. "Once upon a time," he said, "the members of the body resolved that they would no longer support the belly, which did nothing at all, but lay at ease while they toiled. 'We will not carry it,' said the feet. 'We will do no more work for it,' cried the hands. 'And we will not chew a morsel for it, even if food is placed between us,' declared the teeth. They kept their word, and the belly suffered; but they suffered with it, and soon they, too, began to waste away."

The plebeians understood the meaning of the fable. They talked together, and finally they said to the patricians, "We will return to Rome if you will agree, first, to forgive the debtors who cannot pay; second, to free those who have been made slaves; and, third, to have two trib'unes appointed to see that the patrician magistrates do not wrong us." The patricians agreed to these terms, and they and the plebeians made a treaty as formally as if they had been two nations. The hill where this meeting was held received the name of the Sacred Mountain. At its summit an altar was built and sacrifices were offered to Jupiter.

It was not long before the number of plebeian tribunes was

HOW THE PLEBEIANS WON THEIR RIGHTS 37

increased to ten; and, moreover, plebeian æ'diles were also chosen who aided the tribunes and cared for the streets and public records, and superintended the public games.

It was a great gain to the plebeians to have tribunes, but their troubles were not over by any means. Many of them were exceedingly poor, and those whose debts had been forgiven had nothing to make a start with, and were almost as wretched as they had been in the first place. This was all the harder to bear because the patricians had a large amount of property which the plebeians felt ought fairly to be shared with them. This property was in land which had been taken in war. The plebeians said, "We have fought to win the land, and we ought to have a part of it." This was not so easy

AN ÆDILE GIVING THE SIGNAL FOR A CHARIOT RACE

a thing to bring about, because the patricians held possession of it and were not at all inclined to give it up. They cultivated it or used it for pasturage of their flocks and herds as they chose. They were supposed to pay the state for its use, but the collectors were patricians and seldom troubled them. If the owner of flocks and herds can have free pasturage for them, he can hardly help becoming rich. The patricians, then, were growing richer, while the plebeians were growing poorer. The plebeians could not even get employment on the land, for they were liable to be called away to war at any moment; and the patricians naturally preferred slaves who could be kept at their work.

Some, even among the patricians, saw how unfair this was, and one of them, Spu-rius Cas'si-us, proposed that the patricians be obliged to pay a fair rental for the land which they were using, and that part of the state lands be divided into small farms and given to needy Romans and Latins. Then there was anger among the patricians. "Spurius Cassius is trying to make himself popular and become king," they declared; and even the plebeians were not especially grateful, for, although the Latins had become their allies, they did not like the idea of giving them Roman lands. This land law, or A-gra'ri-an Law, may possibly have been passed, but it was never carried out.

VINTAGE FESTIVAL

Nevertheless, the plebeians were slowly increasing in

HOW THE PLEBEIANS WON THEIR RIGHTS

power. Their next gain came about by the passing of a law proposed by the tribune, Pub-lil′i-us. The tribunes had always been elected by the assembly of the centuries. Each century had one vote; but as more than half the centuries were made up of wealthy men, no one who would not be inclined to favor the rich rather than the poor could become a tribune. Publilius proposed that the tribunes be elected by a plebeian assembly of tribes, or meeting of plebeians who were land-owners. In this assembly of tribes which he proposed, every vote would be of the same value. This law was finally passed, and now the plebeians were free to elect their own tribunes. They had nothing to do with making the laws; but if they did not obey those made by the patricians, the tribunes could protect them from unjust punishment.

The Romans had a great respect for law, but the laws of Rome had never been written. An unjust judge could declare that the law said whatever he wished it to say, and the accused man had no way of proving that the judge was false. "Give us written laws," demanded the plebeians. "Put them up in the forum, that every man may know if he is breaking them." The patricians refused this demand, and they continued to refuse it for ten long years. The plebeians persisted, and at the end of that time the patricians yielded. Instead of consuls and tribunes, ten men, the *de-cem′vi-ri*, were chosen to rule the state and also to decide what the laws were. This was done. The laws were engraved on tablets of bronze, and these tablets, the "Twelve Tables," were set up in the forum where everyone could read them. Copies of the laws were made to use in the schools, and every boy had to learn them by heart.

The Romans meant to elect new decemviri each year, but a proud and insolent man named Appius Claudius, grandson of the Appius Claudius who so despised the plebeians, contrived to get himself reëlected and to make the other nine yield to whatever he chose to do. He suspected that a brave old soldier was plotting against him, and he had the old man murdered. He wanted to get possession of a free-born maiden named Vir-gin'i-a, and therefore he declared as a judge that she was the slave of one of his followers. Then her father caught up a knife and plunged it into her heart. "This is the only way," he cried, "to keep you from slavery and shame." With the bloody knife still in his hand, he and a great company of citizens hastened to the army and told the terrible story. Then the soldiers left their generals and marched straight back to the city. Once more the plebeians went forth to the Sacred Mountain; and now Appius Claudius was in terror, for they declared that they would not return unless

DEATH OF VIRGINIA

more power and better protection were given them, and they demanded that he and the other decemviri be burned alive. They finally agreed, however, to return, provided they might have tribunes again. Eight of the "wicked ten" were banished. Appius Claudius and one other committed suicide.

The plebeians had their tribunes; and a little later the "Va-le'ri-o-Ho-ra'tian Laws," so named from the consuls Valerius and Horatius, who secured their passage, gave the tribunes the right to sit at the door of the senate house, listen to whatever went on, and say, *Veto* (*I forbid it*), to any measure of which they did not approve. More than this, they decreed that whatever resolutions the plebeian assembly of tribes passed should become laws. This was in 449 B. C.

The plebeians were gaining in power rapidly. They could pass resolutions which would become laws; they could elect their own tribunes, and those tribunes could listen to whatever went on in the senate house. Before long, they were allowed to marry among the patricians. There was one office, that of consul, which the patricians were determined they should never hold. They did succeed, however, in holding a new office, that of "military tribune with consular power," which was really almost the same as that of consul. The patricians could not prevent this, but they elected some new patrician officers called *censors* and gave them much of the power which the consuls had held. These censors not only numbered the people and took an account of their property, but they had a right to reduce the rank of a man if they decided that he had been cruel to his family, or extravagant, or dishonest, or was in any way unworthy. They could also increase his taxes, for they could set whatever valuation they chose upon his vineyards and olive trees and carriages and jewels and slaves. Indeed, while the censor held office and wore his scarlet robe, he was almost as independent in his way as a dictator.

The plebeians had felt that it was a victory when they had won the right to be military tribunes with consular power, but now that these censors held so much of the "consular power," they kept on with the fight to become consuls; and at last a law was passed which really gave them more power than the patricians, for it decreed that one consul must be a plebeian, and both might be. For a while the plebeians had to keep close watch to hold on to their rights, but by 300 B. C. the struggle had come to an end, and patricians and plebeians had equal rights in the state.

SUMMARY

The authentic history of Rome begins in 390 B. C., but there is a foundation of truth in the early legends.

Rome had an excellent location, but a disunited people. The plebeians suffered greatly in the wars. They seceded to the Sacred Mountain, but returned on the promise: 1, that their debts should be forgiven; 2, that those who had been made slaves should be set free; 3, that two tribunes should be appointed to defend their rights.

The number of tribunes was increased to ten, and plebeian ædiles were also chosen. The plebeians were refused a share in the land taken in war. A law was passed that the tribunes should be elected in the assembly of tribes.

HOW THE PLEBEIANS WON THEIR RIGHTS

The plebeians demanded written laws; and instead of consuls and tribunes, decemviri were chosen to ascertain what the laws were and set up the "Twelve Tables" in the forum.

Enraged at the crimes of Appius Claudius, the plebeians again withdrew to the Sacred Mountain, but returned on being promised tribunes. The Valerio-Horatian Laws gave these tribunes the right to listen to whatever went on in the senate and veto whatever measures they chose. It also provided that measures passed by the plebeian assembly of tribes should become laws. The plebeians were soon allowed to marry into patrician families and to hold the office of "military tribune with consular power." Then the patricians elected censors, who held much of the consular power. The plebeians finally won the right to become consuls, and by 300 B.C. patricians and plebeians had equal rights in the state.

SUGGESTIONS FOR WRITTEN WORK

A plebeian tells how much he suffered from war.

One of the plebeians tells the story of the secession to the Sacred Mountain.

Spurius Cassius explains and defends his law.

V

HOW ROME BECAME RULER OF ITALY

WHILE the plebeians were struggling for their share in the government of the city, and the patricians were doing their best to keep it out of their hands, there was some danger that no city would be left for either of them to govern. They held Rome and a little land around it; but the Latins and the Her'-

ni-cans were their only allies, and all the other tribes of Italy were their enemies. No one would have expected the little settlement on the Tiber to become strong enough to rule Italy, but that is just what was coming to pass.

It took a long while to bring this about and a great deal of fighting; though this fighting was not always what we should call war in these days. Their enemies, especially the Æ'qui-ans and the Vol'sci-ans, were so near that whenever they had a good chance, they made sudden raids upon the Roman lands, did all the damage they could, and then hurried home.

The Romans did the same thing in return. Sometimes there were real battles, and a city was taken by one party or the other.

Not much is known of these wars except that the Romans were finally victorious; but there are two or three fine old stories about them that ought not to be forgotten. One is the story of a valiant soldier named Caius Mar'ci-us. The Romans were besieging Co-ri'o-li, a town held by the Volscians, when the Volscians suddenly threw open the gates and dashed out upon them. The young Caius Marcius and his followers repelled their attack, rushed in through the open gates, caught up firebrands, and set fire to the houses nearest the wall. Then the Volscian women and children wailed, and the men cried out in terror, for they were in the hands of their enemies. In memory of this exploit, the Romans gave the young hero the name of Co-ri-o-la'-

A CAPTAIN

nus, and after this he was known as Caius Marcius Coriolanus.

A little later there was a famine in Rome. Corn was brought from Sicily, and the senators were discussing at what price it should be sold to the plebeians. Coriolanus had from the first been indignant that the plebeians should be gaining power in the state, and he said, "If the plebeians want corn at the old rates, let them give up their tribunes and restore to the senators their own proper rights." The plebeians learned of this speech, and they were so angry that Coriolanus had to flee to the Volscians. He offered to lead them against Rome. They were delighted to have so famous a leader, and he set out with a large army. He took one Roman town after another, and pitched his camp only a few miles from Rome. Then the Romans were in great alarm. They sent some of the senators, old friends of Coriolanus, to ask him to make peace; but he refused. Then the priests went to him, wearing their robes of office and bearing the images of the gods; but he still refused. Suddenly a friend told him that a great company of noble ladies was approaching the camp. "And unless my eyes deceive me," said the friend, "your mother and wife and children are at their head." Coriolanus sprang from his seat. Before him stood his mother, with his wife on one side, and his children on the other. He would have thrown his arms about his mother's neck, but she drew back. "First let me know," she said sternly, "whether I am coming to my son or to an enemy. Is it possible that you can lay waste this land which gave you birth and has cared for you? Look at your wife and children, and think that if you persist, they must either die or become slaves." The whole company of women moaned and lamented and begged him to spare the city. His children and his wife kissed him and embraced him and begged for mercy. At last Coriolanus yielded. He turned to his mother and said sadly, "Mother, this is a happy victory for you and for Rome, but it is shame and ruin for your son." He withdrew his troops and returned to the Volscians. Some say that in their anger they put him to death, and some say that he remained an exile among them as long as he lived.

CORIOLANUS YIELDS TO HIS MOTHER'S PRAYERS

From the wars with the Æquians comes the story of Lucius Quinc'ti-us, called Cin-cin-na'tus, or the curly-haired. He was a patrician, but he was poor, and he and his wife lived contentedly on their little farm just beyond the Tiber. One warm day he had thrown off his toga, and, wearing only his tunic, was busily ploughing when some men from Rome came into the field. They greeted one another in friendly fashion. Then the men spoke to him formally. "Listen to the commands of the senate," they said, "for we are its ambassadors." Cincinnatus wiped off the dust and sweat, his wife brought his toga, and when he had put it on, the ambassadors saluted him with reverence as dictator. A vessel was moored at the river bank, waiting to carry him across to the city. On the opposite shore stood his three sons, his relatives, and friends, and nearly all the patricians of Rome. They were in grievous trouble, for the Æquians had shut up the consul and his troops in a narrow valley, and no one could form any plan for rescuing them. The Romans believed that Cincinnatus was the one man who would know what to do, and therefore they had made him dictator. Cincinnatus knew how to think fast, and before night he had decided upon a plan. He ordered every man in Rome to come to the Campus Martius, with his weapons, food for five days, and twelve long, sharp stakes. At sunset they set out on a rapid march and reached the enemy at midnight. Cincinnatus arranged his men in a line around the camp. "When the signal is given," he said, "let each man dig a trench in front of him and also drive down his stakes." In the morning the Æquians found that they were shut in by a ditch, a palisade, and a line of valiant soldiers, and they were forced to surrender. The dictator set up two spears in the ground and tied a third spear across their tops. This was called a yoke, and under it the whole Æquian army was made to march to show that they had become subject to the Roman people. The consul and his men saluted Cincinnatus and voted him a golden crown of a pound's weight. Then they set off for the city. First came the Æquian leaders, led as captives; then the military standards, and Cincinnatus in his chariot. Behind him marched the army with the spoils of the enemy. There was great rejoicing in Rome. Before every house along the way was a table spread with food; and as the soldiers marched through the city, they feasted and sang songs of victory. Honors were showered upon Cincinnatus; but just as soon as he was free, he laid down the dictatorship and went back quietly to his little farm across the Tiber.

From the wars with the Etruscans comes another good story, that of Ca-mil'lus. These Etruscans were an interesting nation. They built strong walls and dikes and handsome temples. They owned many ships and traded with the peoples who lived about the Med-i-ter-ra'ne-an Sea. They made statues and paintings and jewelry. They were rich and powerful; but their power was growing less, for they had been beaten at sea by the Greeks and attacked on land by the Gauls.

GATE OF AN OLD ETRUSCAN CITY

These Gauls had come into Italy from what is now France, and had taken possession of the country to the north of the Etruscans. Now was the chance for the Romans. The patricians were eager to make war upon the Etruscans, for this was not long after Spurius Cassius had proposed the Agrarian Law, which has been mentioned before, and they were afraid the plebeians would insist upon its being carried out. If they were making war, they would have no time to think about land laws; therefore the Romans laid siege to Ve'i-i, one of the twelve Etruscan cities. They knew how to fight in the field, but they were not wise in conducting sieges, and year after year passed without the capture of the city. Men had to be kept in service the year round, and for the first time wages were given to Roman soldiers. Toward the end of one summer, so the legend runs, the waters of the Alban Lake suddenly began to rise, though no rain had fallen. The Romans were alarmed, for they feared this was a sign that the gods were angry with them. They prayed and they offered sacrifices, but the waters continued to rise. Finally some one heard that a soothsayer of Veii had laughed at the labors of the Romans, and declared it to be decreed by the Fates that Veii should not fall until the Alban Lake was drained. The Romans sent to the Greek oracle at Delphi to ask the god A-pol'lo if this was true, and there they received the same answer. "Let the water out," commanded the oracle, "but not to flow into the sea. Rather make courses for it in your fields until it is spent." Then the Romans bored through the side of the hill and let the water out. They cut through hard rock for three miles and made a tunnel about three feet wide and five feet high. Through this the water flowed, then into courses in the fields until it had been spent. The Romans pressed in through this tunnel, and Veii was taken.

Camillus took one town after another in E-tru′ri-a, the country of the Etruscans, until at length he stood before Fa-le′ri-i. There was every reason to fear that this city would be as hard to capture as Veii had been, for it was built high upon an eminence between two great ravines. One day, however, a man appeared at the tent of Camillus with a little band of schoolboys. "These boys are the sons of the chief men of Falerii," he said, "and I am their tutor. I deliver them up to you, and with them in your power, you can easily force their fathers to surrender." The treacherous man expected to

RAVINE ABOVE WHICH STOOD FALERII

HOW ROME BECAME RULER OF ITALY 51

receive a great reward; but Camillus replied indignantly, "We do not make war with boys. When I win, I win by bravery, labor, and arms." Then he stripped the wicked tutor, tied his hands behind his back, and giving the boys rods, told them to drive him back to the town.

On learning of this, the Fa-le'ri-ans declared that they were willing to surrender to so just and honorable a commander. So it was that Falerii fell into the hands of the Romans. The senate paid special honors to Camillus, because he had taken the city of the Etruscans less by warfare than by justice and good faith. Other cities of Etruria were taken by the Romans, and finally they made a peace of twenty years with the Etruscans.

When the people of Veii had seen that their city was about to fall, they had sent messengers to Rome to ask for peace. The senate had refused. Then one of the messengers had said, "In the Book of the Fates it is written that our city shall fall; but it is also written that if Veii falls, Rome, too, shall be destroyed." The senators had paid no attention to this prophecy, but they were soon to remember it; for Rome was about to fall. The fierce and barbarous Gauls, as has been said, were coming down upon Etruria from the north. The Romans became the allies of the Etruscans; but they did not prove to be especially valuable allies, for when they reached the river Al'li-a, a sudden fright seized upon them and they ran away so fast as to get into one another's way. Some of them lost their heads so completely that they ran to some hostile town rather than toward Rome. This defeat at the river Allia in 390 B.C. was the worst that the Romans had ever known.

The Gauls pushed on to Rome. So few Roman soldiers remained that there was not a hope of saving the city. Most of the people fled; but a few of the strongest young men and senators and their families shut themselves up in the citadel, to hold that if possible, and carry on the Roman name. The old men would not go with them to use up the scanty food. They put on their richest robes, and those who had held office arrayed themselves in the handsome garments worn by victors riding in triumph, and seated themselves in the Senate Chamber on their ivory chairs. The enemy pressed into the forum, and there they saw these silent, dignified old men, as calm and motionless as statues. The Gauls stood gazing half in reverence and half in fear. Then one of them stroked the long white beard of a senator, and the old Roman struck him with his ivory sceptre. At this the Gauls struck blow after blow. They killed every one that could be found, plundered the houses and set them afire.

But the brave young warriors held the citadel, and seven months later, they still held it, for it stood on a steep rock and the Gauls had not found the way to it. At length they discovered the path, and one dark night they climbed up in single file so quietly that the foremost man succeeded in reaching the top without being heard by the sentinels. The Romans, however, had watchmen with keener ears than the sentinels, for a flock of geese had been spared by the hungry people because they were sacred to Juno, and they now set up a cackling. Mar'cus Man'li-us, the commander, sprang from his bed, snatched up his arms, and struck with his shield the foremost Gaul. The Gaul fell headlong, carrying

HOW ROME BECAME RULER OF ITALY 53

'others with him. The Romans hurled down stones and javelins. The Gauls who were not killed fled, and the Capitol was saved.

Soon the Gauls heard that enemies were invading their own country, and they offered to leave Rome if the Romans would give them one thousand pounds of gold. The Romans were obliged to agree, and even when they saw that the weights of the scales were false, they could only complain.

THE GEESE OF THE CAPITOL

Bren'nus, leader of the Gauls, threw his sword into the scales beside the weights and cried insolently, "Woe to the vanquished!" But unexpected help was coming to the vanquished. After the fall of Veii, the enemies of Camillus had caused him to be accused of taking for himself some of the treasures of the place, and he had indignantly left Rome. Now in their time of distress, the Romans who had fled from their city begged him to become their commander and lead them back against the Gauls. "If such is the wish of my countrymen in the Capitol," he replied. The men shut up in the Capitol were glad enough not only to ask him to return, but to elect him dictator. This was how it came about that just when Brennus was saying, "Woe to the vanquished!" Camillus appeared with his force and cried, "Rome is not ransomed with gold, but with steel!" The Gauls were so taken by surprise that they were easily routed.

The Gauls had been driven away, but the houses of the Romans were only heaps of ruins and cinders. It is small wonder that they were dismayed. "Let us go to Veii," they cried, "and make that our home." According to the custom of victors, they had either slain the people of Veii or sold them as slaves, and the vacant city stood ready for them. Camillus, however, finally persuaded them not to desert their homes and the places sacred to the rites of the gods, and they set to work to rebuild the city. The poor plebeians were obliged to borrow money, and soon many of them were in great distress. The good Marcus Manlius helped them in every way that he could. He sold

ROMAN SOLDIERS WITH SHIELDS
(From Column of Trajan)

his property and paid the debts of many poor people. It was whispered that he was trying to win the favor of the crowd that he might be made king, and he was put to death. The Gauls came again more than once, but they were finally so harassed by one Lucius Fu'ri-us Camillus, a nephew of the first Camillus, that they fled, and Rome was free from them. The houses and temples were rebuilt; but there was one loss which nothing could make up, and that was of the old records kept by the priests of what had taken place in the city from year to year. These were burned with the temples, and that is why we have only legends for the history of the early days of Rome. /

Rome had now fought with the Æquians, Volscians, Etruscans, and Gauls; but lying to the southeast was the land of the Sam-ni'tes, and between them and the Romans, war arose. The Samnites were a bold, hardy race of mountaineers. They attacked Cap'u-a, one of the cities founded by the Greeks in Italy; and Capua begged Rome to come to her aid. This war was bitter while it lasted, for the Samnites were almost as strong as the Romans. Rome was glad when peace was made, for she was now having trouble, not with her enemies, but with her old allies, the Latins. They were willing and glad to be friends with Rome, but they did not wish to be under her command. "We are as strong as you," they said, "and where there is equal strength, should there not be an equal share in the government? Let half of the senate and one of the consuls be Latins, and we are ready to call ourselves Romans and take Rome for our fatherland."

The proud Roman senators were angry and scornful. "If

a Latin should be permitted to enter our senate," one of them cried, "I would come with my sword and strike him down with my own hand." War followed. The greatest battle was fought near Mt. Ve-su'vi-us. There is a legend that on the night before the battle each consul dreamed that the side would win whose general should of his own will give his life for his country. Both consuls were eager to sacrifice themselves; but they agreed that the one whose troops first began to give way should be the victim. The troops of De'ci-us Mus were the first to fall back. Then Decius cast his spear upon the ground and, standing upon it, cried aloud, "Ye gods, I beg that you will grant victory to the Roman people; and as a sacrifice I now give myself up to death." He mounted his horse and dashed into the midst of the enemy and was slain.

The other consul, Ti'tus Manlius, made an even greater sacrifice for his country. The two armies were so nearly matched that the Romans needed to take every care. Orders were given that there should be no single combats; but one of the Latins called to the son of Manlius: "Come forth, come forth, and I will show you how much better a Latin can fight than a Roman." The young man forgot his father's commands, galloped forth, and slew his enemy. He and his troop hastened to tell the consul of the victory. But the consul ordered the trumpet to be blown to call the assembly together, and told them of his son's disobedience. "I must forget either the state or myself," he said sadly. Then he ordered his son to be bound to a stake and beheaded. It was by such stern patriotism as this that Rome won her victories.

HOW ROME BECAME RULER OF ITALY

The Latins were obliged to yield, and they waited anxiously to see how Rome would treat them. Rome was exceedingly wise. She made a separate treaty with every city; she allowed them to trade with her, but not with one another; and she promised each city that if its people proved faithful to her, they should some day be counted as Roman citizens.

It was not long, however, before Rome, too, had to meet defeat. The Samnites attacked a town friendly to her. The Roman troops hurried to the rescue, but on the way they were caught by the enemy in a narrow valley called the Cau'dine Forks and were all taken prisoners. The father of

SAMNITE FOOTMAN
(From a Vase)

Ga'vi-us Pon'ti-us, the Sam'nite general, was a feeble old man, but of great wisdom; and Pontius sent a wagon to bring him to the camp to advise what to do with the captives. "There is no middle course," said the old man. "You must either let them go free, and so win the friendship of the Romans; or else you must slay every man of them, and so weaken the Roman state that it cannot harm you." Unfortunately for himself, Pontius did not follow his father's advice, but thought he had discovered a "middle course." He made the Roman consuls agree to a disgraceful peace, took away all arms from the troops, and sent the whole army under the yoke.

When the Romans heard of this, they put on mourning, closed their shops, and postponed their festivals. "Such a treaty must never be kept," they declared. "No consuls had any right to make it." "Either keep it or else put your troops back into the valley," retorted the Samnites. "Their weapons shall be given back, and we will see how the matter will end." The Romans refused, and so the war went on. Before long Pontius found that the advice of his father had been wise; for the Romans won a decisive victory, captured Pontius, and put him to death. At length the Samnites had to yield.

The peace with the Samnites did not last long, for the Romans were becoming so strong that the Gauls and Etruscans gladly united with the Samnites to try to conquer them. At Sen-ti'num the Romans in 295 B.C. won a decisive victory, although it was five years longer before the resolute Samnites sued for peace.

It was now plain that Rome was to be mistress of Italy. Even the wealthy Greek towns in the south were under her rule except Ta-ren'tum, and with that she had a treaty. One of the terms of this treaty was that no Roman vessel should enter the harbor of Tarentum. One summer noon the people of the place were sitting in their theatre. The seats ran up the hillside and gave a view of the bay. Suddenly the whole audience left their places and hurried to the shore, for they had caught sight of ten Roman vessels sailing toward their city. The Ta-ren'tines had an excellent navy and were good sailors. They sailed out to meet the Romans, and it was not long before they had sunk four Roman ships and

HOW ROME BECAME RULER OF ITALY

taken many captives. When envoys were sent from Rome to demand an explanation, the Tarentines insulted them and laughed at the mistakes they made in trying to talk Greek. War followed. The Tarentines persuaded Pyr'rhus, king of E-pi'rus, to come to their aid. Fortunately for him, he brought twenty elephants with him. Neither the Romans nor their horses were accustomed to elephants, and Pyrrhus won the battle of Her-a-cle'a in 280 B. C. Nevertheless, the Romans fought so bravely and Pyrrhus lost so many men, that he declared a few more such victories would ruin him. He sent to the Romans his most eloquent ambassador to discuss making peace. The Romans would have yielded to his request had it not been for one Appius Claudius Cæ'cus, a man who had formerly been consul and also censor.

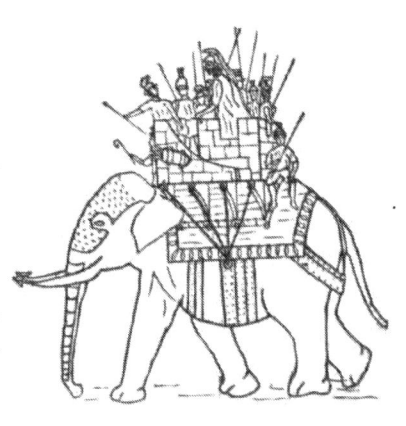

WAR ELEPHANT

He was now old and blind; but notwithstanding this, he entered the senate and in a burning speech begged the senators never to make peace so long as Pyrrhus was in Italy. The envoy of Pyrrhus returned to his master. "The Roman senate is an assembly of kings," he declared. Still, Pyrrhus did not give up at once. He spent two years in Sicily, helping the Greek colonies of the island against the Car-tha-gin'i-ans of northern Africa; then he met the Romans at

Ben-e-ven'tum in 275 B. C., and was so completely overcome that he had to return to Epirus. Tarentum yielded, and soon the other Greek cities fell into the hands of the Romans. An Italian "city" meant not only the town itself within the walls, but also the district surrounding the town, so that in conquering the Italian cities Rome had conquered the whole country. From the "toe" of Italy to the tiny rivers Ru'bicon and Ma'cra, the whole land was in the power of the Romans.

SUMMARY

From the wars with the Volscians comes the story of Coriolanus, who spared Rome at his own peril. In the wars with the Æquians, Cincinnatus was called from the plough to save the state. During the long siege of Veii, wages were paid to the Roman soldiers for the first time The Romans drained the Alban Lake, entered Veii through the tunnel, and captured the city.

Camillus punished the treacherous schoolmaster, and the Falerians surrendered.

The Romans went to the aid of the Etruscans against the Gauls, but were defeated at the river Allia. The Gauls entered Rome, but the warning of the geese saved the citadel. Camillus, who had been exiled, returned and ransomed Rome "with steel." Rome was rebuilt.

The Romans fought with the Samnites and the Latins. The battle of Mt. Vesuvius is noted for the sacrifice of Decius Mus. Manlius punished his son's disobedience with death. Rome conquered the Latins and made a treaty with each city separately. At the Caudine Forks, the Romans were sent under the yoke; but soon avenged themselves by a victory.

The Gauls, Etruscans, and Samnites united to conquer the Romans; but the Roman victory at Sentinum, in 295 B. C., made it clear that Rome was to be mistress of Italy.

Contrary to their treaty, the Romans entered the harbor of Tarentum. War ensued. The Tarentines, aided by Pyrrhus and his elephants, won the battle of Heraclea, in 280 B. C., but with such losses that Pyrrhus wished to make peace. The Romans refused, and Pyrrhus was driven back to Epirus. From the "toe" of Italy to the Rubicon and the Macra, the whole land was in the power of the Romans.

SUGGESTIONS FOR WRITTEN WORK

The wife of Cincinnatus describes the visit of the ambassadors to her husband.

One of the schoolboys of Falerii tells the story of Camillus and the treacherous schoolmaster.

A Gaul tells his friends of the coming of Camillus to ransom Rome.

A Roman soldier describes his first sight of the elephants of Pyrrhus.

VI

THE ROMANS OF THE EARLY REPUBLIC AND THEIR WAYS

EVEN if there were no truth in the old stories of Rome, they would, nevertheless, tell us much about the character of the Romans. People are always inclined to become like those whom they admire, and therefore the best Romans must have been like the heroes of the legends. They were, then, dignified and somewhat stern in manner, with great respect for the law and strong love of country. So long as the father lived, the son must yield to him in all private matters; but as a citizen the son was free, and if he happened to hold a higher office in the state than his father, the father must show him due honor. There is a story that a famous old general, Fa'bi-us Cunc-ta'tor, had a brilliant son who was made consul. This office put him at the head of the army, and the father was, therefore, under him. The general rode up to greet his son as usual, but the son bade him dismount before he ventured to address a consul. The old general whom all Rome delighted to honor was greatly pleased and said, "My son, I wished to see whether you would remember the respect due you as consul of the Roman people."

In the earlier times, the Romans lived very simply. Their houses were at first a single room with a hole in the roof to let the smoke out, and a hole in the floor to drain off the rain that leaked in through the roof. The walls were black with the smoke that did not go out. This room, the *a'tri-um*, was the living-room of the home. Here the wife and her daughters spun and wove. Here was an altar with images of the ancestors of the family who were worshiped as household gods, and were supposed to protect the home. Here were a table, a bed, a hearth for the open fire, and not much besides. Up to the time when Tarentum was captured, even those who were well-to-do lived in houses that had simply added to this atrium a few rooms for sleeping, although as Rome increased in wealth and power, the houses of the rich grew more spacious and more elegant.

THE ROMANS OF THE EARLY REPUBLIC 63

The food was as simple as the house. The early Romans ate peas, beans, onions, and other vegetables, and a sort of porridge made of wheat; but meat was not often used.

The dress of a Roman consisted chiefly of a *toga*. This was a long oval scarf, perhaps ten feet wide. It was folded lengthwise and draped over the left shoulder, under the right, and over the left again. One end hung down in the back, while the other was tucked into the fold or loop in front. Arranging the toga was an important matter. A man would have been laughed at from one end of the town to the other who ventured out into the streets with his toga draped over the right shoulder instead of the left. Under the toga, the Roman wore a tunic, or kind of shirt without sleeves. If the weather was cold, he put on one or two extra tunics, and perhaps a sort of mantle. Hats were not worn unless a man was traveling and the sun was uncomfortably warm. In the house the Roman wore sandals on his bare feet, but for the street he had shoes somewhat like those of to-day. The tunic and toga were made of white woolen cloth, but members of the senate were allowed to

ROMAN IN A TOGA
(From a Statue in the Museum at Naples)

have a broad purple stripe running down the front of the tunic. Slaves wore tunics and sometimes, in cold weather, cloaks; but they were never permitted to wear the toga, for that was regarded as the special dress of the Roman citizen. The Roman boy wore a toga with a broad purple border until he was about seventeen. Then his father and a company of friends led him to the forum to enroll his name as a citizen, and after this he was permitted to wear the "manly toga," as it was called.

The Roman woman wore a tunic and vest, and over these another tunic long enough to touch the floor. This was the *stola*. It was kept in place by a girdle. When the Roman lady went out of doors, she put on a *palla*, or shawl of white woolen, draping it in much the same fashion as the toga of the men.

Children were sent to school, usually in the care of some trusty slave who was to see that they behaved well in the streets. It is not probable that in early times they learned much of books besides reading, writing, and a little arithmetic; but they were taught to ride, swim, and use arms, in order that they might be of value in defending the state, and they were most carefully trained to be honest and truthful, to worship the gods, to love their country, and above all things to be strictly obedient. If a child dis-

A ROMAN LADY
(From a Marble Statue Found in a Roman Tomb)

obeyed his father, the father might sell him as a slave or even put him to death. If a man broke the law of the state, his fellow-citizens thought he had forfeited all right to live.

The Romans believed that the spirits of the dead lingered around their tombs. If these spirits received due honor from their descendants, they were happy and kept loving watch over the home. If they were neglected, they were miserable and became mischievous and dangerous.

SCHOOL OF VESTAL VIRGINS

Le Roux

The goddess of the hearth was Vesta, and the fire on the hearth was her symbol. Each family paid respect to Vesta at their own fireside; but besides this, a public temple was built in her honor, and there six maidens watched her sacred fires that they might never be permitted to go out. The Romans worshiped Jupiter as father of the gods. The god of war was Mars; the god of property and commerce was Her'cu-les. These four were the principal gods of the early Romans, but there were hosts of others. There was Juno, wife of Jupiter; Neptune, god of the waters; Mi-ner'va the wise; Ve'nus the beautiful; the two-faced Janus, whose temple was open in war and closed in peace — indeed, there was a god for every action. When a Roman was about to carry his corn into the barn, he offered a sacrifice to the god of carrying corn into barns and prayed that he might do it successfully.

The worship of the Romans was practiced as a sort of barter between themselves and the gods. They believed that if they did not worship the gods, some evil would come upon them; but that if they offered up prayers and sacrifices, they would get favors. They thought that it was especially pleasing to the gods to watch athletic games; and therefore if a Roman magistrate wished to make sure of good harvests for the people, or if a military commander was in danger of defeat, he would promise the gods that if they would help him, he would celebrate games, or athletic contests, in their honor, such as wrestling and racing. When any important business was to be undertaken, the *augur*, who interpreted the will of the gods, was always consulted. He went to some high place, prayed, and offered up sacrifices, then seated himself with his face to the east to watch the sky. There were many fixed rules for interpreting what he might see or hear. For instance, it was a good

JUNO
(In the Ludovisi Villa, Rome)

sign if a raven croaked on the right; but if a crow appeared, it must croak on the left to bring good luck. Thunder on the left was fortunate for everything but holding the comitia. A flight of birds in one part of the sky was favorable to any proposed plan, but in another part, unfavorable. There were other omens than these appearances in the sky. To spill salt or stumble or sneeze was sure to bring bad luck unless the suppliant made some gift to the gods to ward off their displeasure.

In celebrating a marriage, the augur was always called upon to "take the *auspices*," that is, to watch the various omens and see whether they were favorable. This was done before sunrise, for the wedding ceremonies required a whole day. The guests came together at the house of the parents of the bride and listened eagerly while the augur reported what he had seen, and explained its meaning. Then all eyes were turned upon the bride

A ROMAN AUGUR

and bridegroom, for the words of marriage were now to be spoken. The bride wore a snow-white tunic. Her hair had been parted into six locks with the point of a spear, and over it was thrown a red veil. After the words of marriage had been said, some woman friend of the bride's family led the couple to the altar. They walked around it hand in hand

and offered up a cow, a pig, and a sheep. Then the guests cried, "*Feliciter! Feliciter!*" that is, "Good wishes!" or "May you be happy!" and the feast began. At nightfall the bride pretended to cling to her mother, while the bridegroom tore her away and carried her to her new home. This show of force was perhaps in memory of the stealing of the Sabine women in the days of Romulus. The journey to the home of the bridegroom was not a solitary one by any means, for anybody followed who chose. Torch-bearers led the procession, men played on flutes, and the people sang songs. There were always many boys in the company, for the bridegroom carried a supply of nuts to scatter among them. This was to show that he was throwing away all childish things. At the threshold the bride paused, for there the evil goddesses called the Furies were supposed to dwell. If she were to stumble, it would be a most unlucky omen; and therefore she was always lifted into the atrium. On the following day the wedding guests came together again, for now it was the turn of the bridegroom to give a

A ROMAN BRIDE

THE ROMANS OF THE EARLY REPUBLIC 69

feast. The household gods were not forgotten, and the bride offered a sacrifice to them to show that she was now a member of her husband's family and joined in the worship of his ancestors.

It is no wonder that the Romans wanted the gods to favor their enterprises, for they undertook works of great magnitude. As has been said before, they did not hesitate to set to work to drain a lake by means of a tunnel, the building of which would be no small undertaking even with modern machinery. The Cloaca Maxima, the great sewer built by Tarquinius Priscus, is twenty-five centuries old and still does its work. They built channels under ground and mighty aqueducts on lofty arches above ground to bring fresh water into the city. In the reign of Tarquinius Priscus, they built the Circus Maximus, — a race-course in a valley, with seats rising in tiers on the slopes of the hills. This was large enough to hold many thousand spectators. The Romans were also famous builders of roads. If a city came under their rule, they immediately

FESTIVAL IN HONOR OF FLORA, THE GODDESS OF FLOWERS

CHARIOT RACE, CIRCUS MAXIMUS

built a direct road to it. The most famous of the Roman roads is the one leading from Rome to Capua. It is called the Vi′a Ap′pi-a, or Ap′pi-an Way, because it was built while Appius Claudius Cæcus was censor. The roadway was first covered with broken stone and cement; then upon this were laid exceedingly large blocks of hard rock, cut so smooth and square that the pavement seems almost as if made in one piece.

The one aim of the Romans was to make Rome powerful; and the chief object of these roads was to enable them to march bodies of soldiers to any given place without delay. Therefore they did not trouble themselves to search out easy grades for their roads; they made them as straight as possible. If a valley was in the way, they built lofty viaducts across it. If a mountain stood before them, they dug a tunnel through it. If it had not been for these roads, the Romans could never have held Italy under their rule; but every conquered city knew that at the suspicion of a revolt, the terrible

THE ROMANS OF THE EARLY REPUBLIC 71

Roman troops would come down upon them, and that the punishments of Rome were swift and severe.

Another method by which Rome kept her conquests was by a much pleasanter means than fighting or threatening, that is, by founding colonies. When Rome overcame a district, part of the land was always given to Roman citizens who would go there to found colonies. These colonies were not mere military camps; they were founded by men who had come to live quietly on their farms. They governed the colonies as Rome was governed, and they practiced the manners and customs of Rome. The result was that the conquered people soon learned to talk Latin and to understand Roman ways of living and thinking and ruling. Just as far as possible the Romans made it difficult for these conquered towns to have much to do with one another, but easy to have dealings with Rome. As their people came to know more of Rome, they could hardly help learning to admire her and wishing to become citizens. So it was that Rome held fast whatever country came into her hands. It is wonderful that a tiny settlement surrounded by enemies should have been able to grow into a state strong enough to overcome all these enemies. It is still more wonderful that having overcome them, she should have succeeded in making them not only obedient to her rule, but proud of being governed by a city that they had come to look upon with respect and admiration.

SUMMARY

The old stories of Rome give a good idea of the character of the people. The houses and the food were simple. The toga was the chief article of the man's dress, the stola of the woman's. Children were taught to know a little of books, to use their bodies well, to worship the gods, to love their country, and to be obedient.

The Romans had many gods. Their worship was a sort of barter between themselves and the gods. The augur was the interpreter of the will of the gods and of the significance of omens. The wedding ceremonies required a full day.

The Romans were famous builders. The chief object of their roads was to enable them to march bodies of troops rapidly. Rome kept her conquests by force and by founding colonies.

SUGGESTIONS FOR WRITTEN WORK

Fabius Cunctator tells the story of saluting his son.
A Roman school-boy tells what he likes best to do.
A Roman describes the omens seen by an augur.
A description of a wedding procession.

VII

HOW THE ROMANS CONQUERED CARTHAGE

ITALY is shaped like a boot, and the toe of the boot points across Sicily and the Mediterranean to Africa where the city of Car'thage once stood. Carthage was founded about one hundred years earlier than Rome. The land about it was most fertile, and it had an excellent harbor. The Carthaginians were famous merchants, and they had a large number of trading vessels. They loaded these with gold, ivory, linen, precious stones, and slaves from Africa; embroideries and purple cloth and glass from the eastern coast of the Mediterranean; iron from the little island of El'ba; wax from Cor'si-ca; gold from Spain; and oil and wine from Sicily; and these products they carried from port to port. Chiefly through this trading, Carthage had become wealthy: her rule extended over all northern Africa to the westward, and over several large islands; southern Spain paid her tribute; her trading posts and colonies were so thickly scattered over the Mediterranean shores that the Carthaginians declared this sea to be only a Carthaginian lake, wherein no one might venture to wash his hands without their permission. They could well defend their claims, for they had, besides trading vessels, a powerful navy of warships.

Just between Carthage and the "toe" of Italy lies the island of Sicily, only ninety miles from the African shores. The Carthaginians traded with Sicily, and finally planted colonies on the western coast. On the eastern coast were some Greek colonies, settled soon after the founding of Rome. The Greeks were traders as well as the Carthaginians, and the two peoples carried on a constant warfare. In the midst of this enmity, some military adven-

CARTHAGINIAN FOOT SOLDIER

turers from Italy took possession of Mes-sa'na (Mes-si'na), the Si-cil'i-an town nearest Italy. The Greeks attempted to drive them away, and the Italians asked the Romans for aid. "We are Mam'er-tines (sons of Mars)," they said, "and you, too, are descended from Mars. We have come for help to our brothers." The Romans did not wish to help these pirates; but if aid was refused, they would ask the Carthaginians to become their allies, and Messana would become a Carthaginian town. That would never do, declared the Romans; and so

SLINGERS IN CARTHAGINIAN ARMY

the first war with Carthage began. Carthage had been founded by Phœ-nic'i-ans, whom the Romans called Pœ'ni. Therefore the wars with Carthage were known as the Pu'-nic Wars.

For nearly twenty years the Romans had paid no attention to their navy, and they were now almost without warships. They borrowed a few from the Greek colonies in southern Italy and succeeded in landing troops on the shores of Sicily. It was not easy to win a victory over the Romans, and they were as successful in Sicily as elsewhere. They began to dream of more than winning a few Sicilian cities and taking some land and treasure. Why not go on and conquer the whole island? There was one extremely good reason "why not," and that was their lack of warships. While they were in Sicily, the Carthaginians had been sending their ships of war along the Italian coast, and what the Romans had gained in Sicily they had lost at home. Moreover, even if they captured the island, they could not hope to keep it if they had no navy with which to meet the attacks of the Carthaginians. "We must build warships," the Romans declared; but that was more easily said than done, for no one knew how. The ships of war of those days — galleys, they were called — were moved by both sails and oars, but the Romans did not understand how to sail against the wind; therefore, in a naval battle, where it was necessary to move rapidly, they depended chiefly upon the use of oars. The oarsmen sat in tiers, one above another, the higher tier using longer oars than the one below. The Romans could borrow of the Etruscans and the Greeks galleys with two or three banks of oars; but these would be helpless before the Carthaginian galleys with five banks.

People as determined as the Romans can usually find a way out of a difficulty. A Carthaginian warship was wrecked on their coast, and they thought they could make this serve as a model. They began to cut down trees. In sixty days, if we may trust the old story, a forest had been made into a fleet of one hundred and twenty warships. The Romans had not forgotten that the ships must have men; and while the shore resounded with the noise of hammers and axes and saws, soldiers were sitting on tiers of benches, practicing a sort of dry land rowing. At length the ships were ready; but they must have been rather clumsy, and even the rowing practice can hardly have made very skillful sailors.

Probably the Carthaginians laughed scornfully when they had their first view of the enemy's fleet. Probably, too, they wondered why the ignorant Romans came out to battle without lowering their masts, as the custom was, and what could be the use of a queer contrivance shaped like a drawbridge and held up to the masts by ropes running over pulleys. They found out before long; for as soon as a Roman vessel was brought near a Carthaginian galley, down fell the drawbridge, and a heavy spike at the end pierced the enemy's deck, holding the two ships together. Over the drawbridge rushed the fierce Roman soldiers. It was not long before they had taken nearly half the Carthaginian fleet. The rest had fled.

A SEA FIGHT

Then the Romans began to dream of a time when the

HOW THE ROMANS CONQUERED CARTHAGE 77

Mediterranean should be, not a Carthaginian, but a Roman lake. Du-il'li-us, the consul who had won this battle, was most highly honored. The senate decreed that a pillar adorned with the beaks of the ships which he had captured should be set up in the forum in memory of his victory; and that as long as he lived he should be escorted home from evening visits to his friends by torches and music.

The Romans won another great naval victory; then the consul Reg'u-lus led them to the coast of Africa. There they burned and robbed and destroyed. If it had not been for the wisdom of a Greek who was in Africa, Carthage might have been conquered at once. "You have cavalry and elephants," he said to the Carthaginians, "but you try to use them on the hills. Choose a level battlefield and you will win." They begged him to lead them. He did so and won. Regulus was taken prisoner.

Meantime the war was going on in Sicily. The Romans had learned to meet the charge of elephants, and now they not only won a victory by repulsing the animals, but captured them and carried them to Rome. A number of Carthaginian nobles were taken captive in this same battle, and the Carthaginians sent Regulus to Rome to propose an exchange of prisoners and to offer terms of peace. They thought this would surely be brought about because they had made him promise to return if the Romans refused their offers. They did not know how brave and unselfish he was. He did not think it would be for the gain of Rome to exchange prisoners, or to make a treaty with Carthage, and he persuaded the senate not to consent to it. Then he took his last look at his beloved home city, kept his word, and went back to the torture and death that he knew were awaiting him in Carthage.

For twenty-four years the war went on. Then peace was made. The Carthaginians paid Rome a large sum of money, surrendered their prisoners, and gave up all claim to Sicily. Both nations were exhausted, and they were glad to have the war come to an end for a time, but neither expected the peace to last for many years.

REGULUS LEAVING ROME FOR CARTHAGE

The first question for Rome to settle was how to govern Sicily. Up to this time she had used two methods of government for conquered peoples. The Latins she treated almost like equals. She gave them some of the rights of citizens and also the hope that if they were faithful to her, they should some time become full citizens. The other tribes of Italy she allowed to govern their own cities, but required them to be

HOW THE ROMANS CONQUERED CARTHAGE

obedient to her. Sicily she made into what was called a "province"; that is, a district ruled by magistrates sent from Rome. She collected taxes from the islanders, but she gave them no hope that they could ever become Roman citizens.

Rome soon gained a second province, for she forced Carthage to yield Sar-din'i-a and Corsica to her. These she ruled in the same way as Sicily, that is, as if the people were not allies but subjects. She was rapidly increasing in power on the water as well as on the land, and now no one could dispute her rule of the western Mediterranean.

She was also gaining power to the eastward. For a long time the people of Il-lyr'i-a, on the eastern shores of the Ad-ri-at'ic, had been a nation of pirates. If a rich merchant vessel sailed into the Adriatic Sea, it was quite likely to meet a fleet of pirate ships darting out upon it from behind some promontory. These pirates made the I-o'ni-an Sea almost as unsafe as the Adriatic and even attacked the coast cities of Italy and Greece. The Romans broke up this piracy completely, and so won the gratitude of the Greeks.

The Romans now began to think about pushing to the north; and they founded colonies on the land that they had taken from the Gauls long before. They had already built the great road called the Fla-min'i-an Way, and now they extended it much farther north. The Gauls were alarmed, and they made ready to come down upon Rome. Now it was the turn of the Romans to be frightened, for they remembered an old prophecy that some day Gauls would occupy a part of the Roman territory. There is a tradition that to fulfill this prophecy and so make themselves safe, they seized two Gauls and buried them alive in the city. Then they did something decidedly more reasonable; they sent for the troops that were away from Rome, and with their help the Gallic forces were almost utterly destroyed.

In the struggle of Rome with Carthage, Rome had one great advantage;

DYING GAUL
(Sometimes called Dying Gladiator)

namely, most of her soldiers were citizens or hoped to become citizens, and were eager that she should win. The soldiers of Carthage, on the contrary, were hired to fight. They cared little whether Carthage or Rome was the winner, provided they had their pay. After they were sent home from Sicily, there was no pay ready, for the treasury was empty. Then the Carthaginians saw what a mistake they had made in not being as fair as the Romans to the countries that they had conquered, for the soldiers had little trouble in persuading the Carthaginian colonies to revolt. A savage war followed; and if Carthage had not had an especially brilliant general, she might possibly have been destroyed without the attacks of the Romans.

This general's name was Ha-mil'car. He had met the Romans in Sicily, and had fought successfully against them. He was wise as well as brave, and he had insisted upon asking for peace, because he saw that Carthage must have time to train soldiers before she could hope to stand against Rome. Money, too, was needed; and it was decided that the best way to get it was for Hamilcar to go to Spain and gain firm hold of the southern part of the country and also develop the mines of gold and silver.

He was soon ready to start, the augurs declared that the omens were favorable, and he was about to offer up a final sacrifice to the gods when a thought struck him. His little nine-year old son Han'ni-bal was watching the preparations for the sacrifice when his father called him and asked, "Do you wish to go to the war with me?" "Yes," the boy cried eagerly. "Then lay your hand upon the sacrifice," said Hamilcar, "and swear that you will never be a friend to the Roman people." "I swear that I will never be a friend to the Roman people," the child repeated solemnly; and he never forgot his oath.

The vessels set sail for Spain. Hamilcar understood how to deal with the natives, and by his wisdom and kindness more than by warfare, he gained for Carthage the country as far north as the Ta'gus River. Nine years later, he was slain in battle. The Carthaginians would have been glad to give the command of the army into the hands of the brilliant young Hannibal; but he was only nineteen, so they gave it to Hamilcar's son-in-law, Has'dru-bal. Seven years later, Hasdrubal was killed; and now Hannibal, though only twenty-six years of age, was put at the head of the Carthaginian forces in Spain.

Two years later, he felt that he was prepared to conquer Rome. He began by besieging Sa-gun'tum, a Greek colony in Spain. Saguntum had made a treaty with Rome, and Rome sent Hannibal a formal warning not to harass the friends of the Roman people. Hannibal paid no more attention to it than to the wind, but pushed on the siege. The day came when the people of Saguntum saw that they must yield. They meant that the Carthaginians should gain as little as possible by the surrender, so they built a great fire, and into it they tossed all their most valuable possessions. Then in utter despair they threw themselves into the flames.

Of course the Romans did not bear tamely such treatment of their allies. They sent ambassadors to Carthage to demand the surrender of Hannibal and his principal officers. The Carthaginians would not give them up. Then the chief ambassador gathered up the folds of his toga as if something were wrapped in it, and cried, "Here are peace and war; which do you choose?" "Give us whichever you will," was the reply. The Roman shook out his toga, and said, "Then we give you war." "We welcome it with all our hearts," cried several of the councillors.

Hannibal was in Spain meanwhile. He sent for African

HOW THE ROMANS CONQUERED CARTHAGE 83

troops to defend Spain, and despatched Spanish troops to defend Africa. Each army was then among strangers, and it would not be easy for the soldiers to succeed in any possible revolt. After the safety of Carthage and of Spain had been provided for, Hannibal was ready to attempt to conquer Rome. He did not believe that the Romans would ever be overcome by sea fights and attacks here and there upon the coast cities. He thought that it would be far wiser to go from Spain by land and come down into Italy from the north, and so be in the very heart of the Roman possessions. He did not expect to have to meet the forces of Rome without allies, for he believed that the Gauls would be willing to help him, and he thought that although the conquered Italian states would probably be afraid to join him at first, yet they would surely be on his side as soon as they saw that he was on the way to success. With such thoughts as these in mind, Hannibal brought together ninety thousand infantry, twelve thousand cavalry, and thirty-seven elephants, and set off for Italy.

LIGHT FOOTMAN IN CARTHAGINIAN ARMY

Across the river I-be'rus he went and then through the gorges of the Pyr'e-nees. This was rather a slow journey, for he had to conquer as he marched. Beyond the Pyrenees were the Gauls, and they made ready to meet him with arms. He sent envoys to say to their princes, "I shall be glad to receive you in my camp; or if you wish, I will come to yours. I am here as your friend, not as your enemy; and I do not intend to draw my sword until I reach Italy." He presented them with generous gifts, and they willingly allowed him to pass through their lands.

Soon he came to the wide and rapid river Rhone. How should so many thousand men be carried across? This question did not trouble Hannibal in the least. He bribed the people on the right bank to lend him all their boats and even to build more. So the Gauls set to work to make "dug-outs," and the soldiers themselves made all sorts of queer and shapeless craft. No one cared how they looked so long as they would float and carry either men or baggage. On the farther bank was a hostile tribe of Gauls. Hannibal did not wish to do any unnecessary fighting, so one dark night he sent some troops farther up the river. They crossed, and in the darkness slipped around behind the Gauls. In the morning Hannibal kept close watch, and at length he saw the signal of his men, a thread of smoke rising slowly across the sky.

His boats were ready; and soon the savage Gauls were at the water's edge, for the Carthaginian troops were springing ashore from their boats. The Gauls shook their shields above their heads, brandished their weapons, and shouted war songs. Suddenly they heard cries of terror from their rear, for Hannibal's troops that had crossed farther up stream were upon them. With enemies before them and enemies

HOW THE ROMANS CONQUERED CARTHAGE 85

HANNIBAL CROSSING THE RHONE

behind them, they were helpless. They ran away, and Hannibal did not pursue them.

Hannibal pressed on until he was at the foot of the Alps. It is no wonder that his men were terrified at the thought of trying to cross the snow-covered mountains. People from some of the barbarous tribes appeared with wreaths on their heads and waved branches of trees to show that they were friendly. They offered to lead the army up the Alps; and after a while Hannibal concluded to follow them. These false guides led them into a narrow defile where the path was only a ledge with a precipice above and a furious river below. While they were struggling to make their way along the path, the savage people climbed the cliffs above them and rolled down masses of rock. Finally, the army succeeded in getting through the defile. They thought this was as bad as anything could be, but they did not know what sufferings lay before them.

On the ninth day they reached a plain on the summit of a ridge of the Alps. The ground was covered with snow, and it was bitterly cold; but Hannibal stood gazing down upon the Italian plains and felt as if he had already won the victory. "The rest of the way will be smooth and down hill," he said to his soldiers, "and after one or two battles Rome will be in our hands."

HANNIBAL CROSSING THE ALPS

The way was certainly down hill, for the side of the Alps nearer Rome is far steeper than the route by which they had come up. There was no question that it was smooth, for it was over bare ice wet with the slush of melting snow; and the men slipped and slid and tumbled and floundered about helplessly. Then they set to work to build a road — no small task, for it must be strong enough to support the elephants. There were no idlers; the men were working for their lives, and in a few days both men and elephants were in northern Italy.

But meanwhile what had the Romans been doing to defend their country? They had done what they supposed was wise, for they never dreamed that Hannibal would attempt to march through Gaul and come down upon them from the north. They sent one army to Sicily, thence to Africa; and another under Publius Cor-ne'li-us Scip'i-o to Spain. On the way to Spain Scipio learned that Hannibal had already crossed the Pyrenees, and pursued him as far as the Rhone. There he found that the Carthaginian general was three days ahead. He understood then what Hannibal was planning to do. The Romans now sent troops to northern Italy by rapid marches, for news had come that the Gauls were joining the lines of the Carthaginians.

The two armies met on the banks of the Ti-ci'nus River. The Romans were much troubled; for a wolf entered the camp and escaped, and a swarm of bees settled on a tree beneath which the general's tent was pitched, and they feared that these were omens of evil. The Carthaginians, on the other hand, were happy and eager for battle. Their commander had taken his stand before them, promising them land and money and citizenship. After this he had taken a lamb in one hand and a stone in the other, and calling the gods as witnesses to his truth, he had slain the lamb as a sacrifice. Then came the battle of the Ticinus. Hannibal was victorious there and also later on, in the battles fought at the Tre′bi-a River and at Lake Tras-i-me′nus.

The people of Rome were in great distress. Crowds stood at the gates to get the first news from their friends in the army. The senate sat from sunrise to sunset for several days; and while they were in session, word came that Hannibal was winning still more battles. A dictator was chosen, Quin′tus Fabius Maximus. He saw to it that sacrifices should be offered and games and temples vowed to the gods. He strengthened the walls of Rome, cut down the bridges over the Tiber, and also burned the houses and destroyed the growing corn where Hannibal was expected to march. Then he set out to pursue the invader.

Hannibal had meanwhile crossed Italy to the Adriatic shores, and was moving slowly southward, plundering as he went. Fabius did not dare to engage in open battle, for if he lost, Rome could hardly be saved; but he kept close watch of Hannibal, cut off scattered parties of soldiers, and harassed the Carthaginian army in every way possible. The Romans could not have acted more wisely, but the soldiers were almost frantic. Hannibal was destroying their homes, and the dictator would not permit them to strike a blow. They angrily called him "Cunctator," the delayer. They even declared that he was a traitor to Rome. The Roman people believed that they had made a mistake in choosing him as dictator, and they now chose another commander as "co-dictator." This co-dictator attempted a battle; but if Fabius had not hurried to his assistance, the army would have been lost. Then the Romans began to see that Fabius had been wiser than they. They hailed him as savior of his country, and his nickname of Cunctator became a title of honor.

The following year the Romans raised new troops, and now they thought they might venture to meet Hannibal in battle. They had twice as many men as he; but the hitherto invincible Romans had met their match, for at Can'næ in A-pu'li-a they experienced the most terrible defeat that Rome had ever known. Hannibal sent his brother home to Carthage to report the news of the victory. It was so amazing that the Carthaginians would hardly believe him, and to prove his story he poured out a peck of gold rings in the vestibule of the senate house. "These are from the fingers of the Roman nobles who were slain at Cannæ," he said.

There was rejoicing in Carthage, but Rome was almost in despair. The first thought of many was to flee, to leave Rome, even to leave Italy; but the senate closed the city gates. Every one thought that Hannibal would attack Rome, but he did not. One of his officers urged him to do so, but he refused. "You know how to gain a victory, but not how to use one," muttered the officer as he turned away.

Hannibal himself had lost an immense number of men, not only in battle, but by the sufferings and dangers of the march from Spain. He begged Carthage for more men and for money to pay his troops; but his countrymen were inclined to think that if he could win such victories as he had already won, he had troops enough, and that as for gold, so successful a commander ought to be able to capture it from the enemy; therefore they were slow in helping him. He was disappointed that so few of the Italian cities joined him. Capua and Syr′a-cuse were the only places of importance that would form an alliance with him, and the alliance with Capua proved in some ways an injury. He spent the winter within its walls. His soldiers drank and feasted; and when spring came, they were not so ready to continue the war as they would have been in the previous autumn. The Romans, however, would not give him the chance that he wanted to continue the war, for they had become wiser than at first and would not meet him in the open field. They were also becoming stronger; but the longer the Carthaginian army waited, the weaker it became.

TOWER
(It was used by the Romans in besieging a town)

The alliance with Syracuse did not last long, for the Romans soon laid siege to the city. On the land side they moved up wooden towers higher than the city walls, and from these

HOW THE ROMANS CONQUERED CARTHAGE 91

soldiers could shoot, or they could throw out a sort of drawbridge and cross over to the top of the walls. They had battering-rams, — long beams with iron heads, that swung against the walls with terrible force. They also used machines for throwing darts, and others for hurling great stones. On the other hand, the people in the town defended themselves by letting down monstrous pincers to catch

RAM AND TONGS

hold of the Roman battering-rams, and tongs to seize the men who were climbing up on the scaling ladders, and they threw darts and stones and firebrands. On the ocean side was a fleet of Roman vessels which carried wooden towers and battering-rams like those of the land forces. There was small chance for a town besieged by land and by sea; but a wise man named Ar-chi-me′des, who lived in Syracuse, invented many machines to defend the city. The description of one, given by the Latin author Liv'y, who was born a century and a half later, sounds much like a chapter from Jules Verne. According to Livy, this machine acted somewhat like the old-fashioned well-sweep, only instead of a bucket it had a heavy iron grapple. If a ship came a little too near the walls, the beam bent over it, and the grapple caught up its prow, then suddenly dropped it. When attacked in this fashion, the ship usually took in so great a quantity of water as to swamp it. The tradition has been handed down that Archimedes set the Roman fleet afire by arranging mirrors to reflect the sun's rays. In spite of his masterly defense, the Romans captured the city. The Roman commander had great respect for the ability of Archimedes; and to make sure that he would not be harmed, he sent a soldier to bring him to the camp. In the midst of ruin and massacre, the philosopher sat calmly working on a problem in geometry. "Don't disturb my circles," he said to the soldier, hardly deigning even to look up. The soldier was angry

ARCHIMEDES AND THE ROMAN SOLDIERS

HOW THE ROMANS CONQUERED CARTHAGE

and killed him. The Romans also regained Capua. In punishment for its joining Hannibal, they beheaded fifty-three citizens and sold many others as slaves and took away its privilege of self-government.

The loss of Capua was only the beginning of Hannibal's misfortunes. The other cities that had joined him were alarmed when they saw that he did not conquer Italy so rapidly as they had expected, and one after another they began to do their best to induce Rome to pardon them for revolting against her. A second misfortune for Carthage came when the Romans, meeting Hannibal's brother on his way from Spain to Italy with more troops, defeated the troops at the Me-tau'rus River and killed the commander. Third, Publius Cornelius Scipio, son of the Scipio who fought at the Trebia, was sent to Spain. It is said that at that time there was so little hope of success in Spain that no Roman general of reputation was willing to go there; so Scipio, a young man of twenty-seven years, offered himself. However that may be, he drove the Carthaginians out of the country and induced the Spaniards to stand by the Romans.

Meanwhile, little was being done in Italy. The wise men of the olden times used to argue about what would happen if an irresistible force should meet an immovable body. This seemed to be the state of affairs in Italy, with the Romans as the irresistible force and the Carthaginians as the immovable body; for the Romans could not drive out Hannibal, and he could not conquer Rome. Even Hannibal saw, after his brother had failed to reach him with more troops, that he had no further hope of conquest. He had little more opportunity, however, to try to overcome Rome; for the young general, Scipio, was making trouble in Africa, and Hannibal was recalled to that country.

Scipio had by this time concluded that since he had reconquered Spain, the best thing for him to do was to attack Africa. Then, he felt sure, the Carthaginians would be

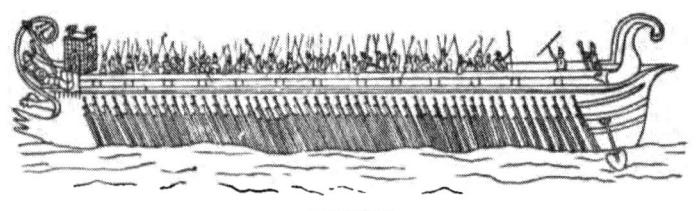

TRIREME
(Galley with three banks of oars)

obliged to send for Hannibal. The senate did not agree with him, and Fabius Cunctator heartily disapproved of the plan. Scipio had become consul, however, and finally the senate yielded, but so unwillingly that they would not grant him a proper number of troops. The common folk had the utmost confidence in him; and when he called for volunteers, they promptly filled up his lines.

Scipio crossed the Mediterranean to Africa and laid siege to U′ti-ca. In those times it was thought fair to trick an enemy in every possible way, and Scipio set to work to persuade some of the allies of the Carthaginians that he was thinking seriously about making peace. These allies were perfectly willing to make peace for themselves, if they had a chance, and desert the Carthaginians. Scipio's real plan was, however, far from making peace; but he was finding out

HOW THE ROMANS CONQUERED CARTHAGE

all that he could about the arrangement of the camps. Then, one dark night, he set fire to the camps of his opponents. They ran wildly from their huts; but the Romans were guarding every way of escape, and the whole Carthaginian army in Africa was destroyed.

It was after this disaster that the Carthaginians ordered Hannibal to bring his troops home to defend their capital. So it was that Hannibal left Italy. He did no good by returning home, however, for he had a terrible battle with Scipio at Za'ma, and this second Carthaginian army was destroyed.

Then Carthage begged for peace. It was granted; but the conquered city was required to pay an enormous sum of money, to agree never to make war anywhere without the consent of Rome, to give up all elephants, prisoners, and deserters, and all ships of war except ten *tri'remes*, that is, galleys with three banks of oars. For seventeen years Hannibal had been trying to conquer Rome, and all his

VICTORIOUS GENERAL THANKING HIS ARMY

struggles had come to nothing but this. The Romans towed the great Carthaginian warships out of the harbor and burned them; and the Carthaginians looked on, grieving as if their city itself were in flames. The deserters were all put to death. The Latins among them were beheaded, the Romans crucified.

Scipio returned to Rome through Italy. All along his way the roads were lined with people who cheered and shouted in their delight that the war was over at last. It was the custom among the Romans for a victorious general to have a "triumph," that is, to ride through the city to the Capitol with a procession of banners, captives in chains, and wagons loaded with the arms and treasures of the enemy. The triumph of Scipio was the most magnificent that had yet been seen. The name Af-ri-ca'nus was given him in honor of his conquest of the Carthaginians.

SCIPIO AFRICANUS
(From a Bronze Bust in the Museum at Naples)

Time passed, and Hannibal showed such ability as a statesman that Carthage soon began to prosper. The Romans were startled and demanded that he should be given up to them. To escape them, he fled from his country and became an exile.

In the two Carthaginian wars, Rome had lost more than

a quarter of a million of her citizens. Hundreds of cities and villages had been destroyed. It had been for so long a time useless to try to cultivate the fields, that great numbers of farmers had given up the attempt, and had crowded into the walled towns. In the midst of so much bloodshed and revenge, the Romans had become far more harsh and cruel than before. On the other hand, Rome had humbled her rival; she had built so large a navy that no nation could oppose her on the sea; and she had gained Spain and overcome Carthage. She had become by far the most powerful of the states of the Mediterranean. Her citizens must have often recalled the prediction said to have been made by Romulus when, after his death, he appeared in a vision: "The gods decree Rome to become the capital of the world."

SUMMARY

The aid given by the Romans to the Mamertines caused the first Punic War in 264 B. C. The Romans built a fleet and captured half of the Carthaginian galleys. Regulus led the Romans to Africa. He refused to urge Rome to make peace with Carthage. Peace was finally made in 241 B. C.

Sicily, Sardinia, and Corsica became Roman provinces. Piracy was suppressed. The Gauls prepared to come down upon Rome, but were routed. The Carthaginian colonies revolted. Hamilcar made Hannibal swear everlasting hatred of the Romans. Hamilcar won for Carthage all Spain to the Tagus. He was followed by Hasdrubal, then by Hannibal. Hannibal conquered Saguntum. The Carthaginians chose war rather than peace.

In 218 B. C., the second Punic War began. Hannibal provided

for the safety of Spain and Africa, then set out for Italy. He crossed the Iberus, the Pyrenees, the Rhone, and the Alps, and entered northern Italy. The Romans had not expected Hannibal to approach from the north, and they had sent troops to Africa and Spain. Learning that Hannibal was in northern Italy, they sent forces to the north, which met him at the Ticinus River, at the Trebia River, and at Lake Trasimenus, and were routed at each place.

Quintus Fabius Maximus was made dictator. He strengthened the walls of Rome, cut down the bridges over the Tiber, destroyed houses and corn where Hannibal was expected to march; and then pursued the invader. Fabius did not dare to meet Hannibal in open battle; and the soldiers angrily called him Cunctator. His policy proved to be correct, and then his nickname became a title of honor.

The Romans were routed at Cannæ in 216 B. C. Hannibal did not attack Rome as the Romans expected. He allied himself with Capua and Syracuse. He weakened his army by a winter in Capua. The Romans captured Syracuse, defended though it was by the skill of Archimedes, and also took Capua. At the Metaurus River in 207 B. C. they overcame Hannibal's brother. Scipio drove the Carthaginians out of Spain, and then attacked Africa, destroying the Carthaginian army in Africa. Hannibal left Italy and brought his troops to Africa, but at Zama they, too, were overcome by Scipio. The Second Punic War ended in 201 B. C. Scipio had a magnificent triumph and received the name Africanus. Hannibal led Carthage to prosperity, but to escape the Romans, he went into exile. In these wars Rome had humbled Carthage and had become the most powerful of the Mediterranean states.

SUGGESTIONS FOR WRITTEN WORK

A boy visits the shore where the Romans are building their fleet.
A Carthaginian tells the story of Regulus.

The boy Hannibal tells another boy of his oath.
One of Hannibal's men sends a letter home describing the descent of the Alps.

VIII

ROME BECOMES THE CAPITAL OF THE WORLD

At the time when the Romans conquered Hannibal, "the world" meant the countries circling around the Mediterranean Sea. In all the lands lying to the west of Italy, the Romans now held the chief power. Toward the east they had already taken one step when they suppressed the pirates of the Adriatic Sea and agreed to protect the Greek cities along the Adriatic coast.

In earlier times Greece could have protected her own cities, but the condition of affairs in the East had changed greatly since those days. About the time when the Romans were subduing the Latins, Al-ex-an'der the Great began his conquests. His father, Philip II, had left him Mac-e-do'ni-a and Greece; but this was a small realm compared with what he meant to win, and he began a wonderful series of victories. When he died, he ruled not only Macedonia and Greece, but also Asia Minor, Syr'i-a, Egypt, Persia, and part of India. This empire was divided among his generals. Possibly Alexander himself could have governed this enormous domain, but his generals could not. They and their successors quarreled and fought, and finally the vast empire broke up into three kingdoms: 1. Egypt. 2. Syria and Asia Minor. 3. Macedonia and Greece.

While the Romans were contending with Hannibal, the king of Macedonia, Philip V., who was an ally of the Carthaginians, attacked some Greek cities which were under the protection of Rome. This led to the First Macedonian War. After Hannibal was subdued, war broke out with Philip again, and with most excellent reason. He and King An-ti′o-chus of Syria plotted to divide Egypt between them. If this plan should succeed, Philip would control the Greek cities on the shores of the Æ-ge′an Sea. A vast amount of trading was carried on in the Ægean Sea, the Black Sea, and the eastern part of the Mediterranean, and from this part of the world came much of the grain needed in Italy. If Philip was successful, then he, an enemy of Rome, could shut off a large part of her food whenever he chose. This was enough to arouse the interest of the Romans. Philip did not trouble himself about what the Romans might think, but attacked Egypt and Athens. The king of Egypt was a boy, and his guardians appealed to Rome for help. As for Athens, that had for some time been an ally of the Romans. Rome warned Philip not to harass the friends of her people. Philip replied that he should prefer peace, but that if they wished to fight, they would learn that Macedonia was as powerful as Rome. Then the armies of Philip and the Romans met in Greece at the Cyn-os-ceph′a-læ, or *dogs' heads*, two ranges of hills facing each other and shaped like the heads of dogs. Philip was thoroughly defeated by the Roman general Flam-i-ni′nus.

Flamininus went to Cor′inth to announce his victory to the Greeks. They were celebrating the Isth′mi-an games in honor of the gods, when the blast of a trumpet was heard, the signal for silence. A herald went forward and proclaimed, "The senate and people of Rome and Titus Quinctius Flamininus, their general, have subdued King Philip and the Macedonians, and do now restore liberty to all states which have been under subjection to King Philip." "Again, again!" cried the people, for some had not fully heard and others could not believe the good news. The herald declared his proclamation a second time. Then from the thousands of joyful Greeks there arose such a shout of joy that, according to an old historian, the crows overhead fell into the theatre from the shock. The games were hurried through. No one cared for them or thought of them, for everybody was eager to come near Flamininus and touch his hand. The brave young general was not accustomed to run from his enemies, but when he saw the whole assembly throwing garlands and ribbons and rushing to embrace him, he did run from them and hid away to keep from being suffocated by his grateful admirers.

Although Flamininus had called Greece free, it was really only free from Philip, and was in the power of the Romans. Antiochus, king of Syria, was not pleased with the result of this war. He was then in Greece, and he declared that he meant to free the Greeks from the Romans. That was easier said than done, and in a short time he was hurrying across the Hel'les-pont to escape from the Roman legions. The brother of Scipio Africanus overcame him at Mag-ne'si-a in Asia Minor, and therefore took the surname of A-si-at'i-cus in honor of his victory. By the treaty of peace which followed, Antiochus had to give up much of Asia Minor to the Romans.

They demanded, also, that he should give up his guest Hannibal, for when Hannibal was forced to leave Carthage, he had fled to Antiochus. Hannibal now made his way to Bi-thyn'i-a; but there, too, the Romans pursued him. When he saw that he could no longer escape them, he poisoned himself rather than fall into their hands. Thus perished Hannibal, one of the greatest generals of ancient times.

Macedonia was not yet subdued, for although Philip had died, his son Per'seus had long been plotting revenge and was eager for a chance to meet the Romans. They met at Pyd'na, and Perseus was defeated. Rome had overcome the East as well as the West, and now Macedonia, Greece, and Asia Minor were in her power.

There were two ways in which Rome might govern her new possessions. One was to send Roman governors to them and make laws for them directly. The other way was to divide them into small kingdoms and let them fight together and weaken one another. Rome followed the second course, and after a while there was always an opportunity for Rome to step in, settle their quarrels, and take the rule herself.

BUGLE PLAYER IN ROMAN ARMY

In conquering these lands, Rome usually claimed that she was giving freedom to the people. They were not always pleased with her "freedom."

THE CAPITAL OF THE WORLD

The people of Corinth, in particular, had no idea of accepting the Romans as rulers, and persisted in making war upon Spar'ta, although the Romans sent envoys to protest against their so doing. The foolish Co-rin'thi-ans hooted and yelled and insulted the envoys in every way, finally driving them from the assembly. One of the leaders made a violent speech, saying that he wished to be a friend of the Romans, but "had no taste for them as masters." It is little wonder that the Roman legions were sent swiftly to Corinth. Then the Corinthians learned what it was to resist Rome and insult her messengers, for the citizens were either killed or sold as slaves, shiploads of statues and paintings were sent to Rome, and enough to load many more ships were destroyed by the soldiers. Then the city was torn down and burned.

The Romans were growing more powerful every day. They were making new conquests, but they did not forget to keep close watch of the old ones. About the time when Corinth began to be rebellious, Mas-i-nis'sa, king of Nu-mid'i-a, attacked Carthage, and Carthage appealed to Rome for help. The Romans sent envoys, but Masinissa was an ally of Rome, and they decided everything in his favor. One of these envoys was Marcus Por'ci-us Ca'to. He was a brilliant commander and he had first been made consul, then censor. He was much troubled because so many of the Romans were giving up the plain, simple ways of their fathers and were beginning to like luxury and to avoid work. Cato cultivated his land with his own hands; he never wore costly garments; and even when he was consul, he drank the same wine as his slaves. He declared once that he could not live with a man whose palate was more sensitive than his heart. When he became censor, the people who liked luxury trembled; and they soon found that they had good reason, for Cato had a list made of the carriages, jewelry, rich clothing, and expensive furniture of each household and its real cost. Then he counted the value as ten times as much and taxed it heavily on that valuation.

This was the man who was sent to Carthage. His eyes were wide open to see all that there was to be seen; and when he returned to Rome, he reported to the senate, "Carthage is not so humble as you imagine. It is a wealthy city; it is well supplied with arms and stores and whatever is needed in warfare, and it is full of men able to bear arms. They are not a weaker, but a more skillful enemy to us than they were." Then he let fall from the folds of his toga some figs that he had brought from Africa, and cried, "Remember that the country in which these grew is only three days' sail from Rome." After this, whenever he made a speech in the senate, no matter what the subject was, he always ended by saying, "And my opinion is that Carthage must be destroyed." Another senator, who did not agree with Cato, always ended *his* speeches in mimicry of him with, "And my opinion is that Carthage must be left standing."

It was not long before the Romans sided with the censor. Naturally, when Masinissa attacked the Carthaginians a second time, they did not call upon Rome, who had failed to defend them and had stood by their enemy, but did their best to defend themselves. They did not succeed, and now they were terrified at the thought of how Rome might punish

THE CAPITAL OF THE WORLD 105

them for breaking the treaty. They sent envoys to Rome to try to excuse themselves and make their peace with her. Rome demanded three hundred boys of the chief families as hostages. These were sent. Then Rome said, "Give up all your arms." Two hundred thousand suits of armor and great quantities of weapons were surrendered. "Tear down your city and make a new settlement ten miles from the ocean," was Rome's next command. The Carthaginian envoys begged for mercy, but Rome rarely showed mercy. The Carthaginians in despair determined to fight to the death. They worked night

CARTHAGINIAN WOMEN
(Preparing for the Romans)

and day to make shields and weapons and engines of war; and even the women worked with them at the fortifications, and cut off their long hair to make bowstrings. When the Romans came to carry out their cruel decree, they found it no easy thing to do. For nearly three years their siege of the city went on. Then Publius Scipio Æm-i-li-a'nus was put in command. He made a line of fortifications across the isthmus which connects the site of Carthage with the mainland, and thus shut off the land supplies from the city. He built a wall across the mouth of the harbor, but the Carthaginians dug a canal and brought out their galleys. He built another wall, he stormed the town and scaled the walls; and even then the starving people resisted so desperately that the Romans had to fight on roofs, on planks and beams, even in rooms. Not until the city was fully in the hands of the Romans, would the fifty thousand Carthaginians surrender who remained alive. These were sold as slaves. The Romans took for the state the immense quantity of gold and silver that remained even then. The soldiers seized whatever they chose of all that was left. Then the town was burned, its site was ploughed up, and it was solemnly declared that a curse would rest upon him who tried to rebuild the city. So it was that Carthage was destroyed, and its territories became a Roman province under the name of Africa with Utica as the chief city.

A SLAVE
(In the Lateran Museum at Rome)

Scipio had a splendid triumph on his return to Rome. Some years later he was sent to Spain, for Nu-man'ti-a had revolted against the Roman sway. For nine years the city withstood a siege, then famine set in and it was obliged to surrender. This city, too, was torn down.

Carthage fell in 146 B. C., and Numantia thirteen years later. The Mediterranean Sea had now become a "Roman lake," for the Romans ruled all the countries around it. These countries made up "the world," as has been said before; therefore the old prophecy had come to pass: Rome had become the capital of the world.

SUMMARY

The vast empire of Alexander was divided among his generals, but finally broke up into three kingdoms, Egypt, Syria and Asia Minor, and Macedonia and Greece.

Philip's attack upon some Greek cities caused the First Macedonian War in 214 B. C. The attempt of Philip and Antiochus of Syria to divide Egypt caused the Second Macedonian War. Flamininus routed Philip at Cynoscephalæ, in 197 B. C., and announced his victory at the games.

Antiochus set out to free Greece from the Romans, but was driven across the Hellespont. He was routed at Magnesia in 190 B. C. At the demand of the Romans that Antiochus should give up Hannibal, the latter poisoned himself to avoid falling into their hands.

The Romans overcame Perseus at Pydna. They then controlled Macedonia, Greece, and Asia Minor. These countries were divided into small kingdoms.

Corinth resisted Rome by making war upon Sparta, and was destroyed by the Romans, in 146 B. C.

The Romans favored Masinissa rather than Carthage. Cato

became a most severe censor. He declared continually that Carthage must be destroyed. Carthage defended herself against Masinissa, and in the attempt to ward off her overthrow at the hands of the Romans, entered upon the Third Punic War in 149 B. C. Carthage was destroyed (146 B. C.).

Numantia revolted and was forced to surrender to the Romans. Rome became the capital of the world.

SUGGESTIONS FOR WRITTEN WORK

Two Romans discuss the plans of Philip and Antiochus.

A boy describes the announcement at the games of the victory of Cynoscephalæ.

Why should Cato tax luxuries?

IX

THE GRACCHI; THE RISE OF MARIUS

No nation is the same at the end of a war as at its beginning. The Romans had been carrying on warfare for a long period, and they were quite different people from the Romans of earlier times. They now tried to imitate the ways of the East, and especially of Greece. It had become the fashion to look down upon everything Roman and to think everything Grecian far superior. The Latin language now seemed to the Romans common and unpolished. They learned Greek and sent their sons to Greece for the last years of their education. They scorned the old simple ways and delighted in the Eastern fashions of living in luxury and spending a great deal of money for amusements.

THE GRACCHI; THE RISE OF MARIUS

The victories of the Romans had brought a vast amount of wealth to Rome, for all the lands that she had conquered were obliged to pay tribute to her. There were new opportunities for men to make large fortunes; for instance, if a man succeeded in getting himself appointed governor of a province, he did not often try to rule the province for the good of the people, but got as much money from them as possible, and it made small difference to him whether by fair means or foul. Then he returned to Rome to try to make more display than any one else. Occasionally, an unjust governor was prosecuted on his return; but this was small gain to the suffering provincials, for now the governors wrung all the more from them to make sure of having enough money to bribe their judges if they were brought to account.

SLAVE MARKET AT ROME

A Roman was no longer satisfied to live on a little farm and till it with his own hands like Cincinnatus; he must own a wide estate and have it cultivated for him. So many wanted these large estates that land became dear, and a poor man could not buy even a small farm. He could not easily get work to do on one of these large places, because most of them were now cared for by slaves. It was a common custom to sell as slaves the people of a conquered city; and the Romans had taken so many cities that slaves had become exceedingly cheap. It was far less expensive to buy them than to pay wages to free men. But how did the poor men live? Some went to the towns and hung upon some wealthy men for their support. Some became soldiers and fought, not to save their country or to strengthen her power, but merely to get their wages and the plunder of conquered cities.

There was little hope of any one's becoming a senator unless he was rich. The Romans were divided into two classes: the rich, who cared for little but display and amusements, and the poor, who were becoming more and more anxious to be idle and luxurious, and who did not care who supported them if they could only get rid of work. The rich were growing richer, and the poor were growing poorer, and both cared chiefly for living idly and comfortably and being amused.

In their amusements the Romans were as stern and cruel as in their warfare. Their entertainments were chiefly the theatre and the gladiatorial combats. Their first knowledge of the theatre came from an educated Greek of Tarentum named Liv'i-us An-dro-ni'cus. When the Romans captured Tarentum, they brought him to Rome as a slave. He learned Latin and translated some Greek plays. This was a new diversion for the Romans. They gave him a building on the Aventine Hill and went in crowds to see him act. From his

THE GRACCHI; THE RISE OF MARIUS

times, the Romans had liked the drama; that is, they liked comedy, and they wanted plays that were amusing and full of jests, often the coarser the better. Tragedy seemed to them dull and stupid; and, indeed, it is no wonder that a man who had seen the destruction of Carthage or Corinth should think a tragedy as acted on the stage a rather tame proceeding.

The Romans had always been stern, and now they had become cruel and often brutal. In the athletic contests they were no longer satisfied with racing and wrestling; they demanded to see real fights and the spilling of real blood. At first they were entertained by watching battles between wild beasts, lions, leopards, panthers, and elephants, sometimes hundreds of them fighting together in the same arena; but this soon ceased to be interesting. Those who are cruel to animals always become cruel to people; and the Romans soon wanted the excitement of seeing *men* fight and die. It was an old custom among the Etruscans to have combats between prisoners at the grave of a warrior. This was introduced into Rome, and the Romans found it so entertaining that they soon ceased to limit it to funerals or to single pairs of combatants. These fighters were called glad'i-a-tors, from *gladius*, the Latin word for *sword*. At first the gladiators were

AN ACTOR
(From a Statue in the Vatican)

all slaves and criminals. Sometimes they were promised freedom if they fought for a certain number of years and were not slain. These men fought savagely, but not always skillfully, and the Romans were soon a little bored by seeing fighting done in a clumsy fashion. Schools were established where gladiators were trained to fight, and from which they could be obtained at any moment. Not only slaves, but some of the wild, reckless men of Rome went to these schools.

"THUMBS DOWN" — *Gérôme*

At the close of a gladiatorial combat, the victor stood proudly beside the vanquished and waited for the spectators to say what should be done with him. If the man had made a brave fight, they stretched out their hands with the thumbs up; but if he had shown himself awkward or cowardly, the

THE GRACCHI; THE RISE OF MARIUS

thumbs were pointed down, and he was put to death on the instant. The citizens who watched the gladiatorial shows year after year became more and more brutal. Toward one another they had to keep up some appearance of courtesy, but they had no feeling whatever for their slaves. These slaves were often of much finer breeding and education than their masters and had been used to living more luxuriously; but when a shipload of them arrived at Rome, their purchaser drove them off in chains to his farm, branded them with his name or mark with red-hot irons, and set them at hard labor. If the work of a slave was not satisfactory, or if his master became angry with him, he was flogged or tortured or even crucified. If he was sick, no one paid any attention to him, for it was cheaper to buy another slave than to care for a sick man. Even the good Cato, who tried so hard to lead the people back

GLADIATORS GOING TO CIRCUS *Saunier*

to the simple ways of their forefathers, looked upon his slaves as little more than machines, and when they could work no longer, he either sold them or turned them off to live or die as they might.

There was also much misery among the freemen of Italy. This was increased by the change from tilling the soil to raising sheep. Sheep-raising needs much land and few workmen. For a long while it had been hard for a poor man to find employment, and it was becoming doubly hard, now that so few workmen were needed. Rome had grown wealthy and powerful, but her citizens were fast becoming idle, extravagant, and dissolute.

Many people were troubled and anxious about this state of affairs, but one man believed that he knew what ought to be done to better matters. This was one of the nobles, Ti-be'ri-us Grac'chus, grandson of Scipio Africanus. His father had died when he and his brother Caius were children, but he had a wise mother, Cor-ne'li-a, who brought up her sons with the greatest care. The story is told that a friend who was visiting her displayed some beautiful jewels and asked to see hers. Cornelia put her off for a little until the children came in from school. Then she said to her friend, "These are my jewels."

Tiberius Gracchus had seen for himself how the poor were suffering because the great landowners held so much land and worked it with slaves. There was an old law that no one should have more than two hundred and fifty acres of the public land; but the poor could not see to it that the law was enforced and the rich would not. Tiberius proposed a new law, which was in reality almost the same as the old one; but there was little hope of its being passed.

The rich men who held vast estates of this public land were indignant. Often the land which they held had been in their families for many years, and they had come to feel that it must be their own. They did not care to remember that if it was not just to take the land in the first place, holding it a long while had not made

CORNELIA AND HER JEWELS

the act any more just. Tiberius was an eloquent speaker, and he pleaded most earnestly for the poor. He said: "The wild beasts of Italy have their caves to retire to; but the brave men who spill their blood in her cause have nothing left but air and light. . . . The private soldiers fight and die to advance the wealth and luxury of the great; and they are called masters of the world, while they have not a foot of ground in their possession."

But no matter how eloquently Tiberius spoke, the senators could not be brought to look at the matter as he did. That was not so very important, for if the ten tribunes, of whom Tiberius was one, agreed to propose this law to the assembly of tribes, or meeting of plebeians who were landowners, there was little doubt that it would be passed. But no law could even be proposed unless all ten of the tribunes desired it. The senators induced one of the ten to refuse to present it. Legally, Tiberius could do nothing more; but he reasoned that when a man refused to agree to so good a law, he was not fit to be tribune, and he induced the assembly to pass a vote putting the man out of office. When the tribune refused to give up his office, then by orders of Tiberius, he was pulled down from his place.

However good this new law may have been, it was exceedingly difficult to carry it out, and, what was worse, Tiberius had broken the laws in passing it. As long as he was a tribune, he was safe; and therefore, although this, too, was illegal, he tried to get himself elected tribune for the following year. The nobles were angry and indignant. They rushed out of the senate house. A riot followed, and Tiberius was slain. Before this, the different parties in Rome had tried their best to get their own way; but this was the first time that they had tried to get what they wanted unlawfully and with violence. If the government of any country allows lawbreakers to go unpunished, or even if the citizens are permitted to uphold the laws by unlawful means, that country is sure to become weak. So it was that the act of kind, honest, mistaken Tiberius Gracchus in 133 B. C. was the beginning of the downfall of the republic.

Ten years later, Tiberius's brother, Caius Sem-pro′ni-us Gracchus, proposed that a law should be passed requiring the state to sell grain to the people at much less than the usual price. Then he won over the merchants, bank-

THE GRACCHI; THE RISE OF MARIUS

ers, and other business men by getting laws passed giving them instead of the nobles control of the courts. The common people and the men whose property was in money were friends of Caius; but the senators, whose property was chiefly in land, were his enemies, for they were afraid he would propose a land law, or agrarian law, like that brought forward by his brother Tiberius. They had good reason to be afraid, for this is exactly what he did do. Then he founded colonies at Tarentum and Capua. No one objected to his founding colonies; but when he proposed that the Latins should have all the rights of Roman citizens, the proud people of Rome were indignant. Before long, there was a riot and Caius was slain.

The brothers were dead, and no one came forward to care for the rights of the poor. The slaves, too, were becoming more and more wretched, if that were possible. In Sicily they were especially miserable, and at length they revolted. They fought like demons, for they knew well that if they were captured, torture and death would await them. Four times they overcame the armies of the Romans; but at last they had to yield. Then followed terrible scenes of suffering. Thousands of these prisoners were thrown from cliffs or were crucified.

The poor freemen of Rome were hardly happier than the slaves, for in that city gold was the only power. No one could hope to win even a just cause in the courts unless he had gold with which to bribe the judges. Ju-gur'tha of Numidia said of Rome, "O city, you would sell yourself if you could only find a buyer."

Jugurtha had good reason to make this speech. Masinissa, king of Numidia, had died and Jugurtha had seized the kingdom. The rightful heirs appealed to Rome for help. Rome sent generals and soldiers to regain the kingdom and punish Jugurtha, but for a long time he found it an easy matter to bribe the generals. At length, however, he was conquered by a commander named Caius Ma'ri-us. He was brought to Rome and had to walk in chains at the triumph of Marius. When the procession was about to ascend to the Capitol, he was thrust into the Mamertine dungeons and left to die of hunger.

This Caius Marius was the son of some hard-working country folk. He entered the army as a young man and was so brave and obedient that his general, the famous Scipio Africanus, began to take special notice of him. One evening some one asked Scipio, "When you are gone, where will the Romans find another general equally great?" "Here, perhaps," replied Scipio, laying his hand kindly upon the shoulder of Marius. The young soldier was too excited to sleep that night. Such words as these, coming from so famous a general, seemed to him like the prediction of an oracle. He pushed onward with all his might, and before long he became a 'tribune. While he held this office, he carried a law that lessened the power of the nobles. Then the common folk admired him. Soon he opposed a law which the common folk wanted, but which he thought not best for them; and now the nobles were inclined to admire him. Both parties began to say, "That young Marius is a bold, sturdy fellow. He does what he thinks best and fears no one."

As an officer in the army, Marius was so wise that the other officers respected him, and so simple in all his ways that the common soldiers loved him. If the soldiers had only dry bread for their dinner, the commander, too, dined upon dry bread. If they were digging a trench or throwing up a bulwark, they often found Marius among them working as hard as they. They wrote to their friends at Rome about the brave and honest general, and when he wished to be elected consul, he had little difficulty in getting the office. He was now at the head of the army, and a strong, powerful army he made it. He trained the soldiers to take long marches, to carry their baggage, and to care for their own food. "Marius's mules," the jesters of Rome called them.

The soldiers needed all the training they could get, for soon the Romans were obliged to carry on war, not to increase their power or to punish rebellious states, but to defend their own state. For many years they had felt no fear of attacks by any foreign nation; but now there came tidings from the north that a vast company of barbarians were

LEGIONARY ON THE MARCH

120   STORY OF THE ROMAN PEOPLE

marching toward Italy. "There are at least three hundred thousand," the rumors said, "and in battle they fight like furies. Their war cries are like the roars of wild beasts, so horrible that no man can describe them."

These barbarians were called Cim'bri and Teu'ton-es. They belonged to the German race whose home had been on the shores of the North Sea and the Baltic Sea. They had wandered southward as far as Gaul, or what is now France, and there they had burned and plundered and killed. Then they had come still farther south. Some Roman forces met them in battle beyond the Alps and were defeated as badly as their countrymen had been at Cannæ. The most mortifying part of this defeat was that a barbarian tribe of Switzerland, that had joined the others, compelled a Roman army to pass under the yoke. At this the Romans were

ROMAN ARMY PASSING UNDER THE YOKE   *Gleyre*

fairly terrified. Barbarians had burned their city once; they might do it a second time. Prayers and sacrifices were offered, and no man who was able to bear arms was allowed to leave Italy. Just at this time Marius returned from his victory over Jugurtha. "Marius will save us," cried the people. "Let us make him consul again." This was contrary to the custom, but the Romans were so alarmed that they thought only of choosing a general who could overcome the barbarians; therefore Marius was elected. He was elected year after year, for the barbarians delayed and the fear of them increased.

At length, in 102 B. C., they started for Italy. Marius had not wasted the time of their delay; he had trained his soldiers more and more perfectly, and had kept them busy digging canals and doing other work, so that instead of growing weak, they had become stronger and more ready for battles. The battles came. Marius defeated the barbarians and destroyed their whole army except sixty thousand, who were sent to Rome to be sold as slaves. In this battle, two companies, or cohorts, of Italians had been so fearless and valiant that as a reward he made them all Roman citizens. Of course he had no right to do any such thing; but "the din of battle was so loud that I could not hear the laws," he said.

When Marius returned to Rome, the people were almost ready to worship him as a god. "Romulus founded our city," they cried. "Camillus saved it, and now Marius has saved it a second time." They were eager to give him whatever he wanted, and he was beginning to think himself so great a man that no honor and no power could be more than he deserved. Just at this time there was another revolt of the slaves in Sicily, and with the same result — defeat, torture, and crucifixion. Before the revolt was fully quieted, there was trouble in Rome, and Marius, stupidly, perhaps, rather than wickedly, united with some men who were trying to overthrow the government. He had been consul five times, but he was eager for even greater honors, and he was not at all particular by what means they might be won. He was the ablest general of his age, but he had no idea how to behave in political life. He seems to have tried to keep free from the crimes of his allies, but to have been more than willing to profit by them. Finally, he became so unpopular that he himself saw that Rome was no place for him. He declared that some time before this he had vowed to offer sacrifices to the mother of the gods, and he set sail for Asia to keep his vow.

HEAD, SUPPOSED TO BE THAT OF MARIUS
(In the Uffizi Gallery, Florence)

THE RULE OF SULLA

SUMMARY

The Romans had lost their old simple ways. Much wealth had come to Rome, and there was a distinct line between the rich and the poor. The chief Roman amusements were the theatre and the gladiatorial combats. The Romans were cruel to their slaves.

Sheep-raising threw many out of employment. Tiberius Gracchus tried to help the poor by limiting the amount of land held by any one person. In the attempt to pass this law (133 B. C.) he resorted to force. This act was the beginning of the downfall of the republic. Later, Caius Gracchus attempted similar reforms, but was slain in a riot. The slaves in Sicily rebelled (133-132 B. C.). Gold had become the only power in Rome. Jugurtha was conquered. Marius rose from the ranks to the head of the army. The Cimbri and Teutones threatened Italy, but were driven away by Marius. The slaves in Sicily rebelled a second time. Marius plotted to overthrow the government.

SUGGESTIONS FOR WRITTEN WORK

A Roman talks about the old customs and the new.

A poor man tells of his sufferings because of the introduction of sheep-raising.

Cornelia's friend describes the "jewel" scene.

X

THE RULE OF SULLA

WHEN Marius returned to Rome, he found the city in difficulties. Thus far, she had ruled the peoples of Italy with a high hand. If she chose to grant privileges to one city and not to another, she did so, and those who were less favored could not help themselves.

The Romans were the only people who had full citizenship. If a Roman was condemned to die or to be flogged, he had the right of appealing to the people. Away from Rome, if a petty Roman officer flogged a non-citizen or killed him, he was in small danger of punishment; but in the farthest corners of the realm, it was a protection to a man to be able to declare himself a Roman citizen. Some years later than this time, a Roman captain in Je-ru'sa-lem bound the apostle Paul and ordered him to be scourged; but one of his officials whispered, "This man is a Roman," and then the captain was greatly alarmed because he had ventured even to bind a Roman.

It is no wonder that the Italians were eager to become citizens. Many of them had fought for the republic, and they thought it only right that they should have a share in the government. Marcus Livius Dru'sus, a tribune, came out boldly and proposed that the Italians be made citizens. The Romans were indignant at such a suggestion, and Drusus was murdered in his own house. As soon as the Italians heard of this murder, they saw that the only way to gain what they believed their rights was to fight for them. They fought with such energy and determination that the Romans were greatly alarmed lest the republic be overthrown. Marius took up arms and overcame them in a great battle. The story is told

STANDARD-BEARER

THE RULE OF SULLA

that an Italian general tried by sneers and taunts to force him to fight when he did not think it best, and called out, "If you are a great general, Marius, come down and fight." Marius retorted, "If you are a great general, make me come down and fight."

When the Romans at last learned that they could not resist all Italy, they yielded, but very grudgingly. First, they gave citizenship to those communities that were not fighting against them; then to all Italians who within two months should declare before a magistrate that they wished to be Roman citizens. This struggle was called the Social War, that is, the war of the *so'ci-i*, or allies. When it was over, nearly all the Italian freemen had become Roman citizens.

Citizenship was a valuable right, but the people who lived in Rome still remained the real rulers, because those who lived away from the city could not often come to Rome to vote. No one had yet thought of having one man chosen to represent each community. The Italians, then, had gained the right to vote, but they could not exercise it; and it must have been most exasperating to have the idlers and vagabonds of Rome make laws for them simply because these idlers lived in the city and they did not.

EAGLE-BEARER IN THE ROMAN ARMY

There was a power in Rome which was fast coming to be above the laws, and that was the army. In the earlier days, every citizen was a soldier when need came. He defended his country as he would have defended his own house, and never thought of demanding pay for the service. At the long siege of Veii the soldiers were kept on duty through the year and could give no care to their crops or business, and therefore, as has been said before, wages were paid them. Under Marius, any citizen might enlist; and now men who had no other way of supporting themselves might always join the army, receive wages, and have a part of whatever plunder might be obtained. They were ready to follow their commander wherever he led, for they knew that if he was successful, there would always be a share in the booty for them. A new master was growing up in the state, for the successful general with his army was more powerful than the senate with the idle, luxurious folk of the capital.

When the army of a state is stronger than the law-making power, there is almost sure to be a struggle between the two for the mastery. The time of struggle in Rome was postponed for a while because of amazing events that had come to pass in the East. Mith-ri-da'tes, king of Pon'tus, kept close watch of what was going on in Rome, and when he saw that the Romans were fully occupied with the Social War, he seized the opportunity to get possession of nearly all the lands bordering on the Eux'ine, or Black Sea, and also to capture some of the Roman lands in Asia Minor. He did not have much time for these exploits, but he did have an exceedingly good opportunity, for the magistrates sent to the countries conquered by the Romans had allowed the money-making Italians who followed them to extort money from the

THE RULE OF SULLA

natives and treat them with such cruelty that they were ready to welcome the rule of Mithridates. Even the Greek cities of Asia were glad to throw aside their allegiance to Rome and claim him as a protector. Athens was so happy in the hope of freedom from Rome that she, too, yielded willingly to this Eastern potentate. When the Social War had come to an end, Mithridates knew that the Roman armies would soon be upon him. "They shall find no friends and helpers here," he said to himself; and by his orders the Italians living in the country were murdered by his officials.

The Romans now made ready an army to punish Mithridates. The senate gave the command to Lucius Cornelius Sul'la, one of the consuls. Sulla had served as lieutenant under Marius in the war against Jugurtha. He had shown a favor to Boc'chus, father-in-law of the usurper, and in return Bocchus had delivered up Jugurtha to the young lieutenant. The honor of the triumphal procession had of course been given to Marius as commander of the army; but so many gave all the glory of the war to the young Sulla that Marius became intensely jealous of him. Sulla had a seal made representing Bocchus in the act of delivering up Jugurtha to him, and used it constantly to seal his letters. Even worse than that, whenever Marius went to the Capitol, he saw gilded figures representing the same scene, which had been presented by Bocchus.

In the Social War and the wars with the Cimbri and the Teutones, Rome had been in such danger that there was no room for jealousy, and both Marius and Sulla had done their best; but this war with Mithridates would bring to the commanding general glory and wealth, and now to have the management of it given to his own former lieutenant was most exasperating to Marius, and he was furiously angry. He was nearly seventy years old, but he went to the Campus Martius, or training ground, every day, and exercised with the young men to prove that he was equal to the toils of a campaign. He persuaded a tribune to propose a law giving to him, instead of to Sulla, command of the army. Now Sulla's soldiers had something to say, for they were devoted to their general. The struggle between the law and the army had begun. The army was victorious, for Sulla led his troops into Rome and drove Marius into exile. Then he set off for the war.

SCREEN OF SHIELDS
(Often used in making an assault. From Column of Trajan)

Marius took refuge on a little vessel and sailed down the coast. He was driven ashore by a storm, and had to hide in the woods to escape horsemen who were searching for him. He begged the sailors not to desert him. "When I was a child," he said, "an eagle's nest with seven young ones in it once fell into my lap. The soothsayers declared this meant that I should be seven times consul. Six times I have held the office; the seventh will surely come, and those who have aided me will not fail of their reward."

THE RULE OF SULLA

In spite of the story of the eagles, the sailors deserted him, and he wandered about through bogs and marshes till he came to a cottage. He begged the owner to save him, and the cottager hid him near a river and covered him with reeds. Soon he heard loud talking and the trampling of horses' hoofs; his enemies were again on his track. He threw off his clothes and plunged into the mud of the swamp. He was discovered and carried into the nearest town. A proclamation had been sent out that he was to be put to death wherever he might be found, and the magistrates sent a man to kill him. The man came back without his weapon. He had rushed into the gloomy cell with drawn sword, but in the darkness he had seen the flash of the old general's eyes and heard a voice demanding solemnly, "Do you dare to kill Marius?" He had thrown down his sword and fled.

Then the people cried out that the man who had saved Italy should be set free. They went to the shore with him and put him on board a vessel. He sailed for Africa and landed where Carthage had once stood; but the Roman governor forbade him to set foot in Africa. "Go and tell him," said Marius, "that you have seen the exile Marius sitting on the ruins of Carthage." A fishing boat was at hand. Marius went on board and fled to a little island off the coast of Africa. Here he heard some good news. The party of the people, led by the consul, Lucius

ROMAN SOLDIER

Cornelius Cin'na, were in power. Marius collected as many volunteers as he could in Africa and in Etruria and appeared at the mouth of the Tiber. He burned and plundered and destroyed. He got possession of the grain that was on its way to Rome, and the starving city was forced to yield.

Then the streets of Rome ran with the blood of her nobles. The heads of consul and senators were fixed to the rostrum, or orator's platform in the forum. Marius was taking a fearful revenge for every insult, every slight. It is said that he walked through the streets with a band of soldiers, and that they killed every man whose salutation he did not return.

The time for the annual election drew near, but Marius and Cinna had put themselves above the law. They did not wait for an election, but simply declared themselves consuls, and no one ventured to contradict them. This was Marius's seventh consulship. He had reached the height of his ambition, but it had brought him neither glory nor happiness. In his long life he should have won a position of honor and hosts of friends. He now held power, but not honor; he had flatterers, but no friends. Sulla would soon return and with him would come a terrible vengeance. Marius was a wretched, miserable old man. He died only a few days after he had seized the consulship.

While Marius was ruling in Rome, his rival Sulla was carrying on the war with Mithridates. Sulla knew that no matter how powerful his enemies might become, yet if he should return from the war a successful general, with ships full of slaves and the treasures of conquered cities, and escorted by a devoted army, he could regain all that he might

THE RULE OF SULLA 131

have lost. He went first to Epirus, then to At'ti-ca, and laid siege to Athens. The Athenians defended their city valiantly; but Sulla had built a stockade about it, and the time soon came when there was no food for even the soldiers. They boiled the hides of oxen, and with the little nourishment that they could get from these, they tottered feebly to the walls and tried to resist the enemy. It was in vain. One midnight Sulla's forces burst into the city. Horns and trumpets sounded, soldiers shouted and yelled and ran through the streets with drawn swords, for they had been commanded to cut down all whom they met, men, women, and children; and then they were free to plunder as they would.

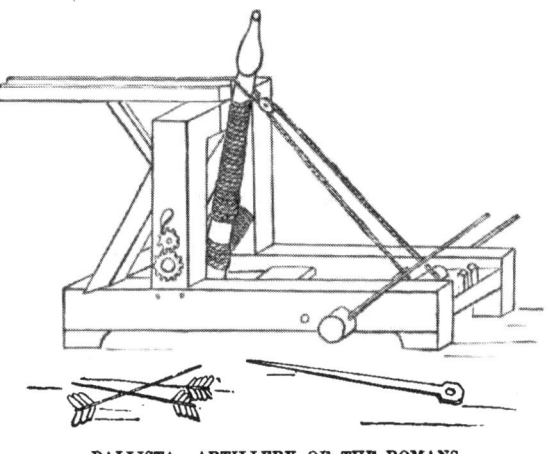

BALLISTA: ARTILLERY OF THE ROMANS
(It was used in besieging cities, and could throw stones weighing 500 to 600 lbs.)

The forces of Mithridates were driven back into Asia, and before long he was begging for peace on the ground that he had once been a friend of Sulla's father! Sulla replied that the king had not recalled the friendship till he had lost one hundred and sixty thousand of his troops. At length, however, peace was made. Cities had been torn down, people had been sold as slaves, and many thousands slain. The king was obliged to give up all the territory that he had seized and to pay a great sum to the Romans.

Sulla was now ready to return to Rome. He sent in advance a long letter to the senate, recounting what he had done for the Roman people. "And in return," he said, "my house has been destroyed, my friends put to death, and my wife and children have barely escaped to me. I shall soon be in Rome to take vengeance upon the guilty." The Romans were terrified, but the senators tried their best to maintain their dignity and sent messengers to say to Sulla that he need have no fear, and if he wanted any protection, he might write to the senate at once. Sulla replied, "I have a devoted army, and I can protect the senate better than it can protect me." Then the Romans knew that he meant to bring his army into the city, and they were more frightened than ever. Their alarm increased, for the Capitol caught fire and burned, and with it the famous Sibylline Books. They had been stored away with the utmost care and fifteen keepers

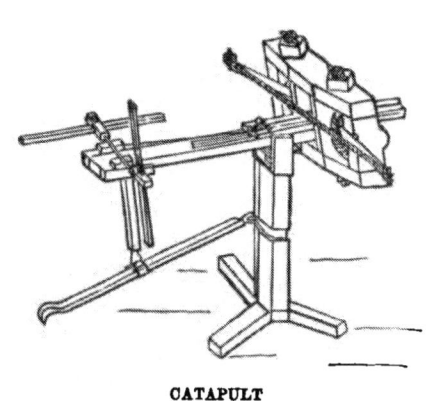

CATAPULT
(A huge bow for throwing sharpened beams, darts, etc.)

appointed to guard them. In times of great danger, the Romans consulted them. They felt sure now that their destruction foretold the overthrow of the city.

They had reason to fear. Sulla landed with his army. The people who had favored Marius opposed him, and the Samnites did likewise, for they thought that this was a good opportunity to revenge themselves for the battles lost in former days to the insolent Romans. There was a great contest just without the city walls. Sulla was victorious and master of Rome. He called the people together and told them that the government would soon go as it ought. His plan for making it "go as it ought" was to kill every one who opposed him. He sold the property of his enemies or gave it to his friends. He slew tens of thousands of Italians who had been of the party of Marius. In Rome itself he had so many persons put to death that a young senator ventured to say to him in the senate, "We do not ask you to spare those whom you have marked out for punishment, but we do beg that you will free from anxiety those whom you have decided to save." "I do not yet know whom I shall save," Sulla replied.

MARBLE HEAD, SUPPOSED TO BE THAT OF SULLA
(In the Vatican)

"Then let us know whom you intend to destroy," besought the senator. Sulla graciously yielded and published a list of eighty names at once. Each day he added to the number. Then he said, "That is all I remember now; the rest must come into some future proscription." These lists were put up in the forum and sent to all the Italian cities. Whoever killed a proscribed man received a reward. It is said that forty-seven hundred citizens of Rome were slain.

Some of the men whom Sulla put to death were enemies of him and his party; some were wealthy, and either he or some of his friends wanted their riches. One young man of eighteen was put on the list because his aunt had been the wife of Marius, and his own wife was the daughter of Cinna. Friends interceded for him, and finally Sulla agreed to spare him if he would divorce his wife. It is said that Sulla spared him unwillingly, saying, "In that boy there is many a Marius." The "boy" would not divorce his wife, but he left Rome for a while. This was Caius Ju′li-us Cæ′sar, who afterward became the most famous of all the Romans.

Sulla meant to rule Rome as he would, but he preferred to have it appear that the Romans had chosen him as ruler. Therefore he went out of the city for a few days, and sent back a letter saying that it seemed to him wise for a dictator to be chosen for an indefinite time until the government should be well established again. He made it clear that he expected to be the choice of the people, and they did not dare to refuse him. Then he set to work to make new laws that should give the senate more authority. He feasted the people for many days, and he gave them a great show of gladiators.

Suddenly he resigned the dictatorship, no one knows

THE RISE OF POMPEY

why, and withdrew to his country house. There he occupied himself with feasting, with companions, both good and bad, with hunting and fishing, with books, the writ-

MOSAIC SHOWING THE CIRCUS GAMES
(Found at Gerona, Spain, in 1884)

ing of his life, and with a close watching of public affairs. A few months later he died. His enemies declared that he should not have the funeral honors usually given to a successful general; but Cnæ'us Pom-pe'i-us, who had been in his army, prevailed upon them to allow it, and his body was borne to the funeral pyre with all the honors that the Romans could pay.

SUMMARY

Roman citizenship was of great value. After the Social War of 91-89 B. C., it was granted to nearly all Italian freemen. The army became the chief power in Rome. Mithridates seized some of the Roman lands. The leadership of the campaign against him was given to Sulla. Marius was driven into exile. After many adventures, he collected an army, returned to Rome, and took a bloody revenge on his enemies.

Sulla captured Athens, but finally yielded to the request of Mithridates for peace. The Romans were in terror at the thought of Sulla's return. The Capitol was burned, and the Sibylline Books were destroyed. Sulla returned to Rome, and took a terrible vengeance on his enemies. By special favor, the life of Cæsar was spared. Sulla was made dictator at his own command. He suddenly withdrew to the country. At his death, he was buried with the honors of a successful general.

SUGGESTIONS FOR WRITTEN WORK

An Italian tells why he wishes to become a Roman citizen.
Marius describes Sulla.
Marius recounts his adventures as a fugitive.
An Athenian child describes the siege of Athens.

XI

THE RISE OF POMPEY

SULLA had declared that the government would soon "go as it ought," but it began to seem as if all things were going as they ought not, for there was trouble in every corner of the republic and in Rome itself. Sulla had brought the senate and the nobles into power again, but no one respected them or their rule. Before he had been dead many months, there was a revolt in Etruria, and the two consuls were sent to settle it. But what would Cincinnatus and Coriolanus and Caius Mucius Scævola and the other old patriots have said to this, — that the consuls were not allowed to set out until they had most solemnly sworn not to permit their armies to fight each other! One of the laws recently passed was that no one should be made consul for two years in succession, but Lep'i-dus, one of the consuls, demanded a second term. This was refused, and then Lepidus and his army made ready to attack Rome; but they were defeated by the other consul and *his* army.

The trouble in the West arose because the people of Lu-si-ta'ni-a, which was nearly the Portugal of to-day, revolted against Rome. They wanted a leader, and they invited a Roman general, Quintus Ser-to'ri-us, to be that leader. He had been on the side of Marius and Cinna, though he did all that he could to prevent their cruelty. When Sulla came into power, Sertorius took refuge in Spain. The natives admired him because he was brave, and they liked him because he was kind and thoughtful. If any of them brought him a gift, however small, he never forgot to show his gratitude. One day a countryman captured a snow-white fawn, so pretty that he carried it at once to the general. This fawn became so fond of him that it followed him wherever he went. The deer was sacred to the goddess Di-a'na, and Sertorius persuaded the people — who

CONSUL WITH WAR CLOAK

were very willing to be persuaded — that this fawn was a gift from her to her favorite. They were glad to obey a favorite of the gods, and Sertorius set to work to form a good government in Spain and teach the people what the Romans had learned. He trained them as the Roman soldiers were trained; and he even opened schools for their children where they could be taught as children were taught in Rome. He often visited these schools and gave rewards to the pupils that had done well.

Many Romans joined him who had fled from the rule of Sulla; he made friends with the Gauls, the Mediterranean pirates, and even with Mithridates; and some people in Rome began to think he was trying to found a rival city. They sent troops against him, but for several years he was more than a match for them. He could always think of some new way of accomplishing what he wished. He once overcame a tribe of savages who lived in caves on a hillside by building up a great mound of dry and crumbly clay. The barbarians laughed and scoffed at him; but when the strong wind began to blow toward the hill, the soldiers galloped up and down on the mound and stirred up a thick cloud of dust. This blew straight into the caves, and after two days the barbarians surrendered.

Sertorius was so strong that at one time the Romans were afraid they had lost Spain. To overcome him they sent the young general, Cnæus Pompeius, now called Pompeius Mag'nus, or Pom'pey the Great, because of his victories over the followers of Marius in Africa and Sicily. Whether Pompey would have succeeded is not known, for some of

THE RISE OF POMPEY

the Romans in Spain became jealous of Sertorius and murdered him at a banquet. Now that the leader was dead, Pompey soon succeeded in making the Roman rule in Spain as strong as ever.

These were the difficulties of Rome in the West; but there were two matters fully as serious as the troubles in Spain and in the East, and they were much nearer home. One was the War with the Gladiators, and the other was the piracy of the Mediterranean Sea.

The War with the Gladiators began at Capua, where there was a gladiatorial school for Gallic prisoners who had been forced to become gladiators. They escaped from the town with only some weapons of the arena which they had seized; but soon they captured some weapons of war from a party sent out from Capua against them. They now numbered forty thousand, for slaves and other gladiators had joined them, and they routed the troops sent against them from Rome. Spar'ta-cus had been chosen as their leader. He very sensibly planned to get away from Italy as soon as possible, so his men could make their way to their homes in Gaul and Thrace. The others, however, had quite different ideas. They had been successful in several engagements, and they had wild hopes of staying in Italy and conquering Rome.

THRACIAN GLADIATOR
(From a Terra Cotta Lamp)

At first the proud senators had felt annoyed and disgraced that a band of barbarians should overpower Roman troops; but now they began to feel alarmed, and they sent both consuls against them. The consuls met with no success. Then they put the war into the hands of the præ'tor Marcus Cras'sus. Spartacus marched toward Sicily and paid some pirates to take him and his army, now consisting of a hundred and fifty thousand men, to the island. The pirates took the money and sailed away without the army. Then Spartacus made himself as strong as he could in Rhe'gi-um. Crassus dug a trench and built a wall across the peninsula upon which Rhegium stands; but one stormy night, Spartacus filled up the trench with earth and wood and passed it with part of his army. He defeated some Roman troops; but this victory was his ruin, for now his men insisted upon meeting the army of Crassus in open combat. They had their way, but were defeated and Spartacus was slain.

Pompey, meanwhile, was just returning from Spain. He met five thousand of the rebels and cut them down. They had learned too late that it would have been wiser to seek the North. The credit of the war belonged to Crassus, but Pompey wrote to the senate, "Crassus has beaten the gladiators in a pitched battle, but I have cut up the war by the roots." When the two generals returned to Rome, both were made consuls; but Pompey was honored with a triumph because of his victories in Spain. According to law, neither Crassus nor Pompey should have been chosen consul; but Crassus was enormously rich and Pompey was a

THE RISE OF POMPEY

favorite among the people. Moreover, Pompey had promised them that if he was elected, he would have a law passed giving back to the tribunes the power which Sulla had taken away.

Sulla had passed another most important law, namely, that a man accused of crime must be tried before a jury of senators. Soon an event occurred which made it possible to repeal this law also. This was the trial of Ver'res, governor of the province of Sicily.

When Rome began to make some of her conquered countries into provinces, she ruled them fairly and kindly; but little by little the rule of the governors had become almost unbelievably cruel and shameless. Verres had taken the greater part of the grain raised by the farmers, sometimes the whole of it. He stole gems, statues, paintings, tapestry, gold and silver vessels, even columns from the temples. No one in Sicily could hold an office or win a cause without making extravagant presents to this infamous governor. The farming lands of Sicily began to look like deserts, for the farmers would not cultivate the ground to have their crops taken away from them. The temples and the finest houses were as bare of their former handsome furnishings as if they had been stripped by a band of robbers. Far worse than this were his terrible cruelties, shown not only to the helpless Sicilians, but to Romans. He dared to imprison Romans without a trial, to scourge them, to put them to death, even by the slave's death of crucifixion. The Roman's great protection, "I am a Roman citizen," counted for nothing with him.

Verres knew that at the end of his three years of office he would probably be brought before the courts; but that did not alarm him, for he thought he could easily buy up his judges. Indeed, he boasted that there was no reason for him to be troubled; one third of his gains would give him an immense fortune, and the rest he was perfectly willing to use to buy his acquittal. Unfortunately for his schemes, the Sicilians engaged a young lawyer, Marcus Tullius Cic′ero, who had once held an important office in their island, to prosecute him. Cicero drew a vivid picture of the sufferings of the Sicilians, the cruelty and wickedness of Verres. Then he began to call out witnesses. Long before they had all testified, Verres saw that his case was hopeless. He took as much of his wealth as possible and fled to Mas-sil′i-a (Marseilles). The corruption of the senate jury was shown so plainly that few could venture to oppose the law providing that one third of a jury should be composed of senators, but the other two thirds should always be of merchants and other men of standing.

All this time a third war with Mithridates was going on, but with little success to the Romans. There was another trouble, however, nearer home, and that was the piracy in the Mediterranean Sea. It had become a real business. The pirates were masters of four hundred cities. They owned a thousand galleys, many of them gorgeous in purple canopies and gilded sterns. They went about boldly with music and feasting, and not only captured ships, but robbed the most sacred temples. They had no respect for the title of Roman citizen, but made raids upon the land and carried

THE RISE OF POMPEY 143

away even officials in their robes of office. The Romans had been so occupied by the wars on land that they had paid little attention to the water, and the pirates had grown so bold that no vessel would venture to sail on the Tus'can Sea.

Then the Romans began to arouse themselves. Italy had come to depend upon Sicily and Africa for much of her grain; and there was danger of famine. What should be done? It was decided to put the whole matter into the hands of Pompey, and to give him for three years the power of a dictator over the Mediterranean Sea and for fifty miles inland. He was to have as much money as he wished, to fit out five hundred galleys, and he was to raise an army of a hundred and twenty-five thousand men. The people were so sure that he would be successful that the price of provisions fell that very day.

They had put their trust in the right man. Pompey divided the Mediterranean Sea into thirteen parts and sent a squadron to each. Within three months the pirates and their strongholds had been captured. Mercy to prisoners was not common in those days, but instead of putting his twenty thousand captives to death, Pompey scattered them among the small towns of Ci-lic'i-a. They were made welcome by the inhabitants because he was wise enough to give each town a large addition of land.

The Romans were overjoyed at this victory, and many of them began to say, "Pompey would bring the war with Mithridates to an end. Let us put him in command." The tribune Caius Manilius formally proposed to do this. Julius

Cæsar supported him, and Cicero made a brilliant speech in favor of the Ma-nil'i-an Law, as this proposal was called. Some of the Romans shook their heads. "No general has ever held so much power," they said; but the law was passed, and while Pompey was still in the east, he was made commander of all the forces outside of Italy. He had the authority to make peace or war with any nation.

This war with Mithridates had begun more than twenty years earlier. Peace had been made twice; but Mithridates had taken up arms again, for he had brought together an excellent army and he believed that he could become ruler of Asia. He certainly had good reason to think that the Asiatic peoples would welcome him, for under the Roman rule they were most miserable. Sulla had inflicted upon them so enormous a fine that to pay it they had been forced to borrow of the Roman money-lenders. The collectors had added interest upon interest, and although the poor people had paid the amount twice over, these collectors claimed that they owed six times as much as the original fine. They had been obliged to strip their temples of the ornaments sacred to the gods, to sell their children into slavery, and even to make themselves slaves to these merciless creditors.

The Romans had sent Lucius Li-cin'i-us Lu-cul'lus to this country to wage war with Mithridates. Lucullus made just laws for interest and taxes and forbade creditors to take more than one fourth of a debtor's income. The moneylenders and collectors were indignant and sent angry protests to Rome. The soldiers of Lucullus did not like him, and when they heard of these protests they mutinied. The Romans did not send him reinforcements, and Lucullus lost the reward of his years of toil. This was the condition of affairs when Pompey was sent to take his place.

Pompey allowed the money-lenders and tax-gatherers to resume their former ill treatment of the natives. Then he set to work to harass the allies of Mithridates. The king was forced to stand alone. His army was destroyed by the Roman leader and he himself barely escaped. Pompey pursued, and Mithridates was driven beyond the Cau'ca-sus Mountains. Pompey made Pontus into a Roman province and subdued Syria and Phœ-nic'i-a and Ju-dæ'a. He besieged Jerusalem, and finally took it by surprising the Jews on the Sabbath, when they thought it wrong to fight. In the temple of Jerusalem he pushed into the Holy of Holies and was much surprised to find no images of the gods there.

MARBLE HEAD, SUPPOSED TO BE THAT OF POMPEY
(In the Vatican)

While Pompey was in these countries, Mithridates was trying to raise an army and follow Hannibal's plan of invading Italy from the north. One day, however, some messengers galloped up to Pompey's camp with a packet. On the points of their spears were crowns of laurel, and the soldiers cried, "Open it, open it!" for the laurel meant good news. They would not wait to build up a mound of turf for a platform, but heaped together a number of pack saddles. Pompey mounted this pile and read aloud, "Mithridates is dead. He killed himself on the revolt of his son Phar'na-ces." Then the soldiers shouted with joy. They offered sacrifices to the gods, and were as happy, says the old historian Plu'tarch, "as if ten thousand of their enemies had been slain."

While Pompey had been subduing the East, Rome had been in a most turbulent condition. The tribunes and the senators were at swords' points; the people hardly knew what they wanted, except that they were bent upon opposing the senate. Law and order had almost vanished, and everything was in confusion. In the midst of this turmoil a conspiracy was formed which nearly destroyed what little government there was left. Lucius Ser'gi-us Cat-i-li'na, or Cat'i-line, made a plot to overthrow the state. He was a reckless young noble, and it was easy for him to find many others who were as deeply in debt as he, and were equally ready to seize upon any means, no matter how dishonorable, to get wealth into their hands. He tried first to have himself elected consul, in order to get possession of some of the revenues of the state; and when he failed, he determined to murder the consuls and other leading men and to burn the city, that in the confusion he might seize whatever he chose. It was not many years before this that the Romans had felt disgraced at having to meet the gladiators in battle, but Catiline planned to invite them to join his army.

It happened, however, that the orator Cicero was con-

CICERO DENOUNCING CATILINE
(From the Fresco by Maccari in the Senate House, Rome)

sul that year. He learned of Catiline's plots, and called the senate together at once in the temple of Jupiter. But when he looked about him, behold, there was Catiline quietly taking his seat among the senators! Then Cicero thundered at him, "In the name of the gods, Catiline, how long will you abuse our patience? Is there no limit to your audacity?" He went on to tell every detail of the infamous plot. When he paused, Catiline tried to clear himself, but there were cries of "Enemy! Murderer!" and he was forced to be silent. Still, the senate was half afraid to seize him, and he went out of the city to his camp in Etruria. He was afterward slain in a battle with the Romans.

Meanwhile, the conspirators who remained in the city were taken prisoners. Cicero now asked the senate to name their punishment. Julius Cæsar thought that their property should be seized and they themselves sent to different Italian cities as prisoners for life. This was a mild punishment for traitors; and when Marcus Porcius Cato, a descendant of Cato the Censor, came to speak, he demanded that they should be put to death. The sentence was executed. The people rejoiced, and when Cicero passed through the forum on his way home, they shouted, "Cicero! Cicero! The Savior of Rome! The Second Founder of the City!" Rome was illuminated; burning torches were placed by the doors of the houses, and women on the roofs held out lamps so that the city should be a blaze of light in honor of the man who had put down so great a conspiracy.

CICERO
(From a Marble Bust in the Museum at Madrid, Spain)

Unfortunately for Cicero, he was never tired of talking and writing about his own deeds. It was the custom that, at the end of a consul's term of office, he should swear that he had obeyed the laws. Instead of following the usual form, Cicero said, "I swear that I have saved my country and preserved the state." The people shouted their applause; but Cæsar and the tribunes were not at all pleased at Cicero's becoming so popular. They proposed a law calling back Pompey and his army to suppress him; but Cato spoke against it so eloquently that instead of wishing to suppress him, the people gave him the title of "Father of his Country." Nevertheless, there were many who did not

THE RISE OF POMPEY

forget that during his consulship Roman citizens had been put to death without a trial.

At the close of the war with Mithridates, Pompey and his army returned to Rome; and such a triumph as he had! In the procession were people from various countries of the East. There were wagons loaded with gold and silver coin, and others without number carrying arms and the beaks of ships. There was the couch of one king, and the throne and sceptre of Mithridates himself. There were great tablets on which were written the names of the kings whom Pompey had conquered and the number of ships that he had taken. There were multitudes of pirates and other prisoners. There were images of those enemies that had been slain, representing them in different battle scenes. The image of Mithridates was nearly twelve feet high and made of solid gold. These came first; then followed the long lines of captives with scores of conquered generals among them. Last came Pompey himself, escorted by his officers. He rode in a chariot blazing with jewels. He wore the cloak of Alexander the Great, "if any one can believe that," the historian Appian says cautiously. There had never been such a triumph before. For two whole days it lasted, and the people of Rome thronged the streets and gazed and gazed. When the procession reached the Capitoline Hill, they expected the captives to be slain according to custom, but Pompey forbade this. With the exception of two kings who were finally put to death, he sent them back to their own countries.

But when the triumph was over, the Romans began to wonder what would come next, for though the people were increasing in power, they had no leader; and the tribunes and the senate were determined opponents.

SUMMARY

There was revolt against the Roman rule in Etruria and in Lusitania. Sertorius became very strong in Spain. Pompeius was sent against him. Sertorius was murdered. The Roman power in Spain became as great as ever.

The War of the Gladiators was put down by Crassus, but the glory of the victory was taken by Pompey.

The outrages of Verres in Sicily were exposed by Cicero, and Verres fled. A third war with Mithridates was going on. Piracy in the Mediterranean was suppressed by Pompey; and to him was given the command of all forces outside of Italy. Lucullus became unpopular, and Pompey was sent to take his place in Asia and carry on the war with Mithridates. He routed Mithridates and captured Jerusalem. Mithridates committed suicide.

The plots of Catiline against Rome were exposed by Cicero. Catiline was slain in battle; other conspirators were put to death. Cicero was hailed as "Father of his Country."

Pompey was honored with a great triumph for having brought the war with Mithridates to an end.

SUGGESTIONS FOR WRITTEN WORK

A speech of Spartacus to the gladiators.

How Pompey captured Jerusalem.

A boy describes Pompey's triumph to another boy living in the country.

XII

CÆSAR AND THE TRIUMVIRATES

THERE were three men in Rome who had made up their minds what should "come next." They were Pompey, Crassus, and Cæsar. Pompey had won such victories that the Romans were proud of him, and he had brought about peace after the long war with Mithridates. He had much power, not only because of the devotion of his soldiers, but because when he had arranged a government for the provinces which he had conquered, he had put friends of his own into all the chief positions.

Crassus was strong because he had an enormous fortune. When Sulla sold the property of his enemies, Crassus bought a large amount of it — very cheap, of course. Then, when houses tumbled down or caught fire, he promptly offered to buy them, and the discouraged owners sold them at a low price. Of his many slaves, more than five hundred were architects and builders, so he could repair the houses at small expense. "He gets his wealth from the troubles of others," the Romans said; but he had a pleasant, obliging manner, and that together with his money gave him much influence in Rome.

The third of these men was Cæsar. He was of an old patrician family, but he had been a follower of Marius, and a most daring one. As has been said before, he would not divorce his wife, Cinna's daughter, to please Sulla; and later, when she died, he pronounced a funeral oration over her, although it was not the custom to do this in the case of young women. He even put images and trophies of Marius into the Capitol. The general's old soldiers thronged into the building to see them and wept for joy. When Cæsar became ædile, he had charge of the public games, and what games they were! He had wild beasts from Africa, captives from the wars, gladiators by the hundred — and a gladiator is thought to have cost about five hundred dollars. This was all done on borrowed money, and when, somewhat later, he was appointed governor of Farther Spain, his creditors demanded their pay so persistently that he appealed to Crassus for help. He received it, for there was something in this extravagant young man which made people believe that he would some day repay them generously for all that they had spent upon him.

CÆSAR
From a Bust in the Museum at Naples

In Spain he was successful in war and he governed well in peace. He treated the natives so much more fairly than they had been treated before that they were greatly pleased with him. He acted as if he were really interested in them, for he made some plans for teaching them Latin and behaved toward them as if they were good for something besides paying taxes. It is said that he went one day into a Spanish

CAESAR AND THE TRIUMVIRATES 153

temple and gazed a long while at a statue of Alexander the Great. "When that man was no older than I," he said, "he had conquered many nations, and I have done nothing."

These three men, Pompey, Crassus, and Cæsar, the First Tri-um'vi-rate, as they are called, bargained together. The first two were to help Cæsar become consul; then he was to pass a law giving land to Pompey's soldiers. This was done. Cæsar wanted an army and a chance to make conquests, and he succeeded in being appointed governor of Gaul for five years. But he did not wish to go from Rome without weakening the power of the senate as much as possible, therefore one of his supporters presented some laws that would do this. There were two men in the senate whom he could not silence, Cato and Cicero. This same supporter brought it about that Cato should be sent away to govern the island of Cy'prus. Next he proposed that any magistrate who had put Roman citizens to death without trial should be forbidden to use fire or water within four hundred miles of Rome. This drove Cicero into exile. Then Cæsar set out for Gaul.

Soon wonderful stories began to come back to Rome from Gaul. Trees were cut down in the forests, and in a few days complicated bridges were built. Great chiefs yielded, towns surrendered. There were tales of forced marches, of surprises, attacks upon the enemy; and with it all the picture of the calm, cool commander who in the midst of a retreat had gently whirled a fugitive around and said, "Friend, you are going the wrong way; the enemy are yonder." There were stories, too, of a mysterious island called Brit'ain across the straits from Gaul, whose white cliffs shone over the water.

Cæsar made only a short visit to this island; but the following year he crossed the straits again and made a number of tribes in the southern part of the island submit to him. He wrote an account of these visits and of his campaigns in Gaul in such clear, simple language that it is a model of military description. The book is known as Cæsar's "Commentaries." Wherever this great man went, he conquered; but after the Gauls had once surrendered, he was so kind that many of them began to wish to learn Roman ways.

Of course Cæsar kept watch on Rome. Crassus and Pompey became consuls, and then the three men arranged matters to suit themselves. Cæsar was to remain in Gaul five years longer. Crassus was to rule the province of Syria for the same length of time; and Pompey was to rule Spain for five years. Crassus was soon slain, and now the world was in the hands of Pompey and Cæsar.

But each wanted the whole world, and just as in the times of Jugurtha, the Roman world was for sale. Pompey began to set tables at which whoever chose might eat, and he gave games and gladiatorial contests. Cæsar sent masses of gold back to Rome to do the same things. Then Pompey induced the senate to let him govern Spain for ten years instead of five. Cæsar was aroused. In five years he would have to return to Rome and disband his army, while Pompey would have *his* army for five years longer. Nothing would be easier than for him to bring about Cæsar's ruin. Pompey had married Cæsar's daughter Julia; but just at this time, she died; so there was nothing to hold the two men together. They no longer pretended to be friends or even to belong to

CAESAR AND THE TRIUMVIRATES

the same party. Pompey stood by the nobles and the present government. Cæsar stood by the people and changes in the government.

Cæsar now asked that he might be made consul; then when he returned to Rome, he would have as much power as Pompey. The senate refused, and commanded him to disband his army. The consul drove out from the senate house the two tribunes who had presented Cæsar's request. This was putting an excellent weapon into his hands, for now he could say to his soldiers, "The tribunes of the Roman people have been insulted. We must take up arms to defend them." He marched on through Gaul to the little river R u'b i-c o n which separated Gaul from Italy. There he paused. To

CÆSAR CROSSING THE RUBICON

pass that stream with his army would be declaring war against Rome, and he might well hesitate. Suddenly he exclaimed, "The die is cast!" and crossed the river.

Then there was wild confusion in the land. Whole cities

fled to Rome, while the people of Rome fled in all directions. "Let every man follow me who prefers his country and liberty to the rod of a tyrant!" declared Pompey, and hastened to Greece. The consuls forgot to offer the usual sacrifices; most of the senators caught up whatever they chanced to touch first in their houses, and they hurried away from Rome.

Before long, various stories of Cæsar's kindness found their way to these terrified people. An old friend of his had gone over to Pompey's side; but Cæsar had sent him his money and equipage. One man in his despair ordered his slave physician to give him poison; but when he learned that Cæsar was merciful, he begged the slave to save him, and was delighted to find that instead of poison the physician had given him only a sleeping draught. The poet Ca-tul'lus wrote a satire against Cæsar, and this new sort of conqueror invited him to supper — and did not poison him.

Cæsar marched on through Italy. City after city yielded to him without the striking of a blow. When he reached Rome, he did not repeat the massacres of Marius and Sulla, but treated people kindly and justly, even those who ventured to oppose him. He had not ships enough to sail directly against Pompey, but he went to Spain, and there defeated Pompey's troops and added them to his own army. Sicily and Sardinia with their vast exports of wheat were soon in his hands. The

LIGHT-ARMED SOLDIER

CAESAR AND THE TRIUMVIRATES 157

following year, he started for Greece. He sailed from Brun-du'si-um across the Adriatic Sea to Macedonia. There was the camp of Pompey, well supplied with arms and food, and with twice as many soldiers as Cæsar had. Nevertheless, Cæsar made an attack. He was repulsed; then Pompey sounded a retreat. "This day victory would have declared for the enemy," said Cæsar thoughtfully, "if they had had a general who knew how to conquer."

Cæsar now withdrew into Thes'sa-ly, and Pompey pursued. On the plains of Phar-sa'lus came the battle which decided who should rule the world. Cæsar's friend Marcus An-to'ni-us commanded the left wing and Cæsar himself the right, where stood his favorite Tenth Legion of tried and faithful soldiers. Pompey had placed his cavalry on his own left wing, opposite Cæsar's right. Cæsar knew that the cavalry was made up of wealthy young men who were not used to wounds and valued their good looks. "Do not throw javelins, and do not strike at their legs and thighs," he had commanded his soldiers of the right wing, "but aim at their faces." He was correct in his judgment of the young cavaliers, for at the first charge, they turned their

ROMAN CAVALRYMAN
(From the Arch of Constantine)

heads and even held their hands up before their faces. Then they ran away as fast as they could go. This ruined Pompey's plans and was the beginning of his total defeat.

Cæsar used his victory mercifully. He pardoned many persons of rank, among them Marcus Brutus. The father of Brutus had been slain by Pompey, but Brutus believed that Pompey's cause was the better, and therefore he had joined the troops of the man whom he abhorred. Cæsar thought so highly of Brutus that it is said he had ordered his men to let him escape if he would not surrender. Pompey had been so sure of success that he had crowned his tents with myrtle, strewn the beds with flowers, and even set bowls of wine upon the tables, that all things might be ready to celebrate his victory. Now he was a fugitive. He drank from a river and spent the night in a poor fisherman's cabin. He had once shown kindness to the father of the boy king of Egypt, and therefore he fled to that country. The king's councillors held a meeting. If they received him, Cæsar would be angry; if they refused, he might some day become powerful enough to punish them, and, moreover, Cæsar might be displeased that they had not delivered Pompey up to him. "The best plan is to invite him to come and then put him to death," urged one of the councillors. "Then you will have done Cæsar a favor, and you will have nothing to fear from Pompey. Dead men do not bite." This advice was followed, and Pompey was slain as he was landing from a boat.

Cæsar had followed Pompey to Egypt, and the bloody head of his enemy was brought to him at once; but the wily councillor had not read him aright. Cæsar turned away in horror, then wept with profound grief and pity. He ordered funeral honors to be paid to the murdered general and afterward punished those who slew him.

In Egypt there was a contest between the boy king and his sister Cle-o-pa′tra for the throne. Cæsar decided in favor of Cleopatra and helped her to establish herself. He then went to Asia, for the son of Mithridates was arousing rebellion against Rome. Cæsar met him at Ze′la and defeated him so promptly that the conqueror told the whole story in three words, "*Veni, vidi, vici*" (*I came, I saw, I conquered*). His opponents had made a last stand at Thap′sus in Africa. He overcame them in a sudden attack. Cato, the unflinching defender of the republic, was in Utica at the time of the battle. The cause was lost, and he would not live to be subject to Cæsar. He fell upon his sword.

A ROMAN TRIUMPH

Then Cæsar returned to Rome. The Romans had thought Pompey's triumph a marvel, but Cæsar's was far more magnificent. Besides the triumph, there were feasts and games and gladiatorial shows and combats of wild beasts. There were gifts to the soldiers and to the poor. There was pardon for those who had been Cæsar's most bitter enemies. The senate named him as dictator for ten years and censor for three years. No Roman had ever held so much power. He was called away for a short time to suppress a revolt of the sons of Pompey in Spain. Then he returned to Rome. The senate could not plan honors enough for him. They made him dictator for life; they gave him the title of "Father of his Country;" they changed the name of the month in which he was born from Quin-ti'lis to Julius (July); they stamped their money with his image; they allowed him to wear a crown of laurel at all times, and at public festivals to robe himself in garments worn by conquerors at their triumphs; they carried his image with those of the gods; they even dedicated temples and altars to him.

In the midst of all this flattery, Cæsar set to work to rule the world as wisely as possible. He made just laws for settling debts; he sent the poor of the cities to live on farms; he gave land to his veterans and settled them in colonies; he gave citizenship to people of conquered countries, not carelessly, but where he was sure it would be appreciated; he reformed the calendar, so that the festivals of the gods would come at the same season each year; he planned a vast collection of Greek and Latin books, magnificent public buildings, the draining of the Pon'tine Marshes, an enormous aqueduct for the city, a survey of the state land, the rebuilding of Corinth and Carthage, a digest or code of the Roman laws, a superb artificial harbor, a road along the Ap'en-nines, and a canal through the Isthmus of Corinth. Enormous wealth had come into his hands, and he spent it freely upon the state.

But there were men in Rome who could not forget that, well as Cæsar was ruling, he had lawfully no right to rule at all, and that the Roman state was no longer a republic. Many believed that he meant to assume the title of king, and the Romans hated the very sound of that word. A conspiracy was made against him. The leaders were Brutus and Brutus's friend Cassius; although to both these men, as, indeed, to almost all of those who joined in the plot, Cæsar had done many favors. On the 15th of March, 44 B.C., the senate met. The conspirators gathered around him as if to offer some petition. At the signal agreed upon, they drew their swords. Cæsar struggled to break through the ring. Then he saw among them Brutus, the friend whom he so admired and loved. He cried, "You, too, Brutus!" drew his robe over his face and fell.

LAST MOMENTS OF CÆSAR

Piloty

Brutus tried to explain to the senators why this deed had been done, and to declare that the old days of the republic were now to return, but they would not hear him. On the following morning they tried to pacify both Cæsar's friends and his murderers by granting to Cæsar the honors due to a god, and also bestowing much power and authority upon Brutus and his followers, whom they made governors of provinces.

Cæsar's friend Marcus Antonius had secured Cæsar's private papers, and now his will was read. His beautiful estate beyond the Tiber was given to the people. Every Roman in the city was to receive a sum equal to fourteen dollars, and generous legacies were left to some of those who murdered him. Marcus Antonius delivered the funeral oration. He showed the people Cæsar's robe, pierced with the twenty-three sword thrusts, and they were wild with rage. They caught up firebrands and rushed through the city to

MARCUS ANTONIUS DELIVERING THE FUNERAL ORATION OVER CÆSAR

find the murderers and burn their houses. Then they went back to the forum to make a funeral pyre. They piled up benches and sticks of wood, and threw upon the heap crowns and trophies and other treasures. All night they stood by the pyre. So it was that Cæsar's body was burned. Meanwhile, Brutus and the other conspirators had escaped from Rome.

Cæsar's soldiers were eager to avenge his death, and at first they sought Antonius as their leader. This was just what he wanted, for he had planned to gain the chief power for himself. Cæsar had made his grand-nephew, Caius Julius Cæsar Oc-ta-vi-a'nus, his heir. This nephew was only eighteen, and when he demanded his rights, Antonius treated him like a troublesome child. Octavianus was hardly more than a boy, but he was wise, and Cæsar's old soldiers liked him. Cicero had been recalled, and in the senate house he made fourteen burning speeches against Antonius. Three hundred years before this, De-mos'the-nes, the most famous of Greek orators, had made some thrilling speeches against King Philip of Macedonia. These were called Phi-lip'pics, and now the same name was given to these orations of Cicero. They influenced the senate to decide in favor of Octavianus. This was the beginning of war between the senate and Octavianus on one side, and Antonius on the other. Antonius had no army, but his friend, Marcus Æ-mil'i-us Lepidus, was governor in Spain and part of Gaul, and he had an army. A battle followed, and Antonius was defeated.

Octavianus was made consul. He then asked Antonius and Lepidus to meet him on a little island in the river Rhine.

For three days these men, the Second Triumvirate, talked and planned. There was much to decide, for they were dividing the world among them. At length they agreed that Octavianus should rule in the West; Lepidus in Africa; and Antonius in the East. They concluded that the only way to make themselves safe was to kill all those who would be likely to oppose them. Hundreds were proscribed, and among them was Cicero. By his efforts, the senate had declared in favor of Octavianus, and the young man had often called him "Father"; but Antonius would come to no agreement whatever unless Octavianus would give up Cicero, and finally he yielded. Lepidus gave up his brother, and Antonius his uncle.

Cicero heard of this proscription, and fled. He went on board a vessel to go to Brutus in Macedonia, then left the sea and walked a long way toward Rome, then took to the sea again, then went to his summer home. Here his servants got him into his litter and carried him toward the sea. But the assassins came upon him, and a few minutes later they had murdered the greatest orator of Rome.

MARCUS BRUTUS
(In the Capitoline Museum at Rome)

Octavianus, Antonius, and Lepidus had slain their enemies in Rome, but Brutus and Cassius had collected a great army in Macedonia, and they must be overcome. Two battles were fought at Phi-lip'pi; Brutus and Cassius were defeated, and both committed suicide.

The Roman world was in the hands of Antonius, Octavianus, and Lepidus; but now Antonius and Octavianus were strong enough to support themselves without Lepidus; and they asserted that he had been plotting to unite with Sex'ti-us, son of Pompey, against them, and he was dropped from the Triumvirate. It was decided that Octavianus was to rule Rome and the West, while Antonius was to rule the East.

Antonius went to the East to put his territories in order. He heard that Cleopatra, queen of Egypt, had given some aid to his opponents, and he commanded her to meet him in Cilicia. She took her time about obeying, and when she ap-

FÊTE AT THE COURT OF CLEOPATRA *Grolleau*

peared at the little river on which was the place of meeting, she came in great magnificence. She was rowed up the stream in a most beautiful galley. The stern was covered with gold, and the sails were of purple silk. The silver oars kept time to the music of flutes and harps and pipes. Clouds of fragrant incense floated down the stream. It is no wonder that the shores were thronged with people, gazing at such a sight as they had never seen before, and every one eager to get a glimpse of the famous queen. She reclined under a canopy most exquisitely embroidered with gold. She was dressed as Venus, and her maids represented the Graces and sea-nymphs. Little boys in the guise of Cupids stood fanning her.

When Antonius met her, he was delighted. She spoke in a sweet, melodious voice. She was witty and fascinating. She pleased and entertained him; and the ruler of half the world spent his time amusing himself with the queen of Egypt. They feasted and hunted and fished together. The story has been handed down that on one of their fishing excursions Antonius had poor success. He was so mortified that he ordered one of his men to dive and fasten to his hook fishes taken from the boat. Cleopatra perceived the trick, and on the following day when Antonius drew up his line, the company shouted with amusement, for she had bidden one of her divers fasten a salt fish to his hook. "Go, general," said she, "leave fishing to us petty princes. Your game is cities, kingdoms, and provinces."

In Rome, everyone was amazed that Antonius should remain in Egypt. They heard that he no longer behaved like a Roman, but like an Eastern ruler. There were even rumors that he meant to make Al-ex-an'dri-a his capital, and from

CAESAR AND THE TRIUMVIRATES

there go forth to conquer Rome. So it came about that Octavianus and Antonius met in battle off Ac'ti-um on the western coast of Greece. Antonius was defeated, and committed suicide. Cleopatra was taken prisoner. She tried to win over Octavianus as she had won Antonius, but did not succeed. She heard that he intended to carry her to Rome to walk in chains at his triumph, and she killed herself. The story was told that she had an asp brought to her in a basket of fruit, and died of its sting. After this, Egypt was a Roman province, and the Roman world was in the hands of one man, the young Octavianus.

SUMMARY

The three great men of Rome were Pompey, Crassus, and Cæsar. In 60 B. C., they formed the First Triumvirate. Cato and Cicero were driven into exile; then Cæsar set out to conquer Gaul. In 55 B. C., he visited Britain. His account of this visit and of his campaigns is called his "Commentaries." The death of Crassus left the Roman world in the hands of Pompey and Cæsar. They became rivals; Pompey stood by the nobles, Cæsar by the people. Cæsar crossed the Rubicon. The Romans fled, but, hearing of his mercy, they returned. Cæsar conquered Italy, Spain, Sicily, and Sardinia. Pompey repulsed him in Macedonia; but by the battle of Pharsalus, in 48 B. C., Cæsar became ruler of the world. He treated his former opponents with mercy. Pompey was slain by command of Ptolemy, King of Egypt. Cæsar made Cleopatra queen of Egypt. He defeated the son of Mithridates at Zela; and at Thapsus, in 46 B. C., he won a decisive victory over his remaining opponents. All the honors of Rome were heaped upon Cæsar, and he made far-reaching plans for the good of the state; but a conspiracy was formed against him, and he was assassinated, 44 B.C. The people and his soldiers were eager to avenge his death.

Antonius schemed for power. He, Octavianus, and Lepidus formed, in 43 B. C., the Second Triumvirate. They proscribed all who would be likely to oppose them. Among those put to death was Cicero.

The triumvirs overpowered Brutus and Cassius at Philippi, in 42 B. C. Lepidus was dropped from the Triumvirate. Antony became ruler of the East. He was fascinated by Cleopatra. It was feared that he meant to make Rome subject to the East. He and Octavianus met in the battle of Actium in 31 B. C. Antonius was defeated, and killed himself. Cleopatra could not win over Octavianus, and she, too, took her own life. Egypt became a Roman province. Octavianus was ruler of the world.

SUGGESTIONS FOR WRITTEN WORK

The crossing of the Rubicon.
The meeting of the Egyptian councillors.
The greatest thing that Cæsar planned to do for the Romans.
The reading of Cæsar's will.

THE THIRD PERIOD
ROME AS AN EMPIRE

XIII
THE REIGN OF AUGUSTUS

CAIUS JULIUS CÆSAR OCTAVIANUS was an exceedingly wise young man. He had seen his uncle lose his life, not because he did not govern well, but because the Romans suspected that he meant to take the title of king. This new ruler believed that it was far more desirable to have power than to have any special title. Moreover, he had learned that a large number of citizens were startled at any suggestion of new laws or abrupt changes, but were contented if the old names and forms of government were kept up. Therefore he called himself simply *im-pe-ra'tor*, a military title meaning hardly more than commander. He never spoke of his victory over Antonius as the triumph of any party, but merely as the successful ending of an Eastern war. He was made consul; and he voted in the senate just as any consul might do. He wore no royal robes, but the ordinary dress of a Roman. His house was like the dwellings of other men of good position, but not pretentious in any way. The people believed that the government was moving on in the old fashion, the senators held their regular meetings and felt that they were deciding all important matters; and yet, little by little, the control of every division of the government was coming into the hands of Octavianus.

Apparently, he held his power with a loose grasp. Sometimes he would offer to give up some of it. Surely, there was no reason to be jealous of a ruler who seemed to have no ambition but to do his best to govern well; and so he came to be at the head of one branch of the government after another. He became censor; *prin'ceps*, or first senator; and pontifex maximus, or chief priest. Finally, he was given the title of *Au-gus'tus*, or the *Majestic*, the *Revered*, and it is by this title that he is usually spoken of in history.

AUGUSTUS PONTIFEX MAXIMUS

Sex-ti'lis, the name of the month in which his first consulate began, was changed to August in his honor.

By this quiet way of controlling the state, the clear-headed imperator, or emperor, was able to bring about what he wanted. One thing that both he and his people wanted was

THE REIGN OF AUGUSTUS

peace. He was obliged to carry on warfare to some extent during his reign, but he did not attempt to make the empire larger. He believed rather that Rome had as wide a dominion as she could well govern, but that it ought to be bounded by mountains, rivers, deserts, or seas, that is, by natural boundaries. As far as possible, he carried out this scheme. He would have liked to take the Elbe for part of the northern boundary; but the German tribes south of that river rebelled, and the Roman army under Va'rus was utterly destroyed. This almost broke the emperor's heart. It is said that he used to cry out in agony even in his dreams, "O Varus, Varus, give me back my legions!" The Rhine and the Danube became the northern limits of the empire; and if a line be drawn from the mouth of the Rhine to Cape St. Vin'cent in Portugal, and that line be moved on to the southeast until it has gone beyond Syria and Egypt, the boundaries so marked will include little that was not under Roman rule.

To make the most of what Rome already held was Augustus's aim. A glance at the story of the dishonest governor, Verres, shows how badly the provinces needed attention and help. Augustus gave these generously. The newer and less peaceful provinces he kept in his own hands. He appointed a governor for each, paid him a salary, and forbade the oppression of the natives. If a governor disobeyed, he was punished. The other provinces were left in the hands of the senate, but they were not forgotten, for Augustus kept close watch of their governors and saw that the provincials were fairly treated. He was always ready to listen to any complaint from them. After the Social War, a man in Italy or in the provinces who had been made a Roman citizen, had a right to vote, but in reality he was ruled by the people who lived in Rome, as has been said before, because they alone could conveniently be present at the assemblies. Now that Augustus had become the one power in Rome, it was gradually coming about that the citizens in Rome had no more power than those hundreds of miles away, for the emperor ruled them all.

The Romans thought it an important part of a ruler's duty to amuse them, and this duty Augustus never neglected. Unfortunately, their favorite amusement was the gladiatorial contest. The emperor made most liberal arrangements for this. He provided wild beasts by the hundred and gladiators by the thousand. "Bread and the games of the circus!" was the cry of the people of Rome, and the state supplied both. The laws of Caius Gracchus, passed more than a century earlier, allowed every Roman citizen to buy grain of the state at half price or less. The privilege had been continued, and the number who depended upon this

THE PANTHEON

THE REIGN OF AUGUSTUS

charity had increased until in the time of Augustus it is probable that fully half of Rome received their food or part of it from the government. Of course some of these people were not able to earn their support; but the others deliberately preferred to ask bread of the state rather than earn it. There was the same old desire of the poor to avoid work; and with it went the eagerness of the rich to find new luxuries.

Augustus was interested in architecture, and he put up many temples, for men were forgetting their old reverence for the gods, and he wished to do all that he could to restore it. Anyone walking through the city would see handsome buildings, such as the Capitol, the *Pan'the-on*, or temple of all the gods, the senate house, and *ba-sil'i-ca*, or hall of justice. There were now several handsome forums in the city; and these public squares, as well as the temples, were adorned with statues. There were beautiful parks and public gardens, and along the Campus Martius were porticoes, whose roofs

A PERFECT COPY OF AN ANCIENT COUNTRY HOUSE
(The Casino del Ligorio, Vatican Gardens)

were upheld by columns, and here people might walk in the shade. On the Palatine Hill were the luxurious homes of the wealthy; but the city as a whole must have been a vast collection of little houses and shops, with lanes, rather than streets, winding in and out among them.

The homes of the wealthy were most splendid. Even those that were in town were so surrounded by gardens and trees

WOMEN'S COURT IN THE HOUSE OF A WEALTHY ROMAN *Boulanger*

and vineyards that one within them might fancy himself many miles away from a city. The houses were full of luxury and gorgeousness, even though they were not always in the best of taste. The vestibule was often adorned with busts and statues, perhaps brought from some conquered city.

THE REIGN OF AUGUSTUS

The walls were painted with some bright color and frescoed. There were tables veneered with plates of gold, silver, or ivory, chairs of cedar, floors of marble or of mosaic work, couches on which to recline at meals, sometimes of bronze, and sometimes of wood inlaid with ivory or gold. The beds had silver legs, mattresses stuffed with down, silken pillows, and richly embroidered purple coverlets. There were beautiful ornaments, vases, and exquisite work in glass. There were most graceful lamps of terra cotta, bronze, or gold.

At their meals the Romans loaded the table as nations do that have more money than good taste, and a slave who could cook perfectly was worth one thousand times as much as an ordinary slave. Vegetables, eggs, fish, fowls of many sorts, peacocks, and wild boars roasted whole, pastries and fruits were used; but the Roman idea of a luxurious meal was one at which many strange dishes appeared. The farther these were brought and the rarer they were, the more deli-

THE CUP OF FRIENDSHIP *Coomans*

cious they were supposed to be. A dinner of six or seven elaborate courses followed by much drinking of wine was not thought to be a sufficient entertainment for guests, and they were amused by rope-dancers, conjurers, and singers.

To learn Greek was so much the fashion that a Greek slave was usually chosen to attend boys to school that he might talk with them in his own language. They learned chiefly reading, writing, and arithmetic. In the reading class, the boys repeated together after the teacher, first the letters, then the syllables of a word, and finally the whole word. The books were of parchment folded into leaves or scrolls of *pa-py'rus*. The text had been copied on them by slaves. When it was time for the writing lesson, the boys took their tablets covered with wax and followed with a sharp point, or *sti'lus*, the letters that the teacher had traced. When they could do this well, they were allowed to make letters on the wax for themselves; and when they could write fairly well, they were promoted to use pens made of reeds, ink, and paper made from papyrus. Arithmetic they learned from an *ab'a-cus*, on whose wires little balls were strung. When the boys grew older, they attended more advanced schools, and in these the masterpieces of Greek literature were taught. Then many of them went on further and studied oratory. They must have Greek teachers, and those who could afford the expense went to Greece to complete their education.

The emperor was interested in literature, and the greatest of all the Latin writers lived during his reign. They were Vir'gil, Hor'ace, Livy, and Ov'id. Virgil, or Publius Virgil′i-us Ma′ro, wrote a long poem, the *Æ-ne′id*, or story of Æneas and his coming to Italy after the fall of Troy. The Romans had been so well pleased with his shorter poems that when they heard of his plan to write the Æneid, they were delighted. They had a long time to wait before seeing the book, for Virgil was not at all strong, and it was seven years before it was half done. Then the emperor asked him to read what he had written. He read first about the night when the Greeks slid softly down from the wooden horse and Troy was taken and burned; then he read about Æneas's stay in Carthage; and last, about his visit to the land of the dead. Here, the poem says, was the young Marcel′lus, whom the fates would "only show to the earth" and then snatch away.

VIRGIL
(Enlarged from a Gem)

"Fling lilies with o'erflowing hands, and let
Me strew his grave with violets,"

Virgil repeated. Marcellus was the name of a favorite nephew whom the emperor had adopted to be his successor. The young man had died only a little while before this, and the emperor was grateful that his name had been made immortal by the poet. In his will, Virgil directed the *Æneid* to be burned because he had not yet made it as perfect as he wished, but Augustus forbade that such a thing should be done. He gave the manuscript to three friends of Virgil, all of them poets, telling them to strike out any phrase that they thought Virgil would have omitted on revision, but to add nothing. So it was that the *Æneid* was saved.

Horace, or Quintus Horatius Flac'cus, had studied in Greece, according to the fashion, and when a young man, had fought in the army of Brutus. Virgil introduced him to Mæ-ce'nas, a wealthy statesman who knew how to be a warm friend. Through Mæcenas he met the emperor, and here he was sure to find appreciation. He wrote no lengthy poem, but many short ones, graceful odes to Mæcenas, to Virgil, to the emperor, to the state, to a beautiful fountain. He understands so well how people feel that one might almost fancy his poems were written yesterday. He thoroughly likes a jest or an unexpected turn. In one poem, a usurer, or money-lender, tells how he longs to live in the country. "Happy is the man," he says, "who dwells on his own farm, far away from the troubles of the city. He can train his vines, or graft his trees, or shear his sheep, or lie

URNS FOR THE ASHES OF THE DEAD
(Found in a Roman Tomb. They are richly carved in white marble)

on the soft grass and hear the birds sing and the little streams murmur." Then Horace ends, "So said the money-lender. He called in all his money on the fifteenth of the month to buy a home in the country — but he forgot the country and loaned it again on the first of the following month." When Mæcenas was dying, he said to Augustus, "Take care of Horace as if he were myself"; but Horace lived only a few months longer than his good friend.

Livy, or Titus Livius, liked to think and talk of the days before the aristocratic notions of the Romans were overthrown by Cæsar, and Augustus playfully called him a follower of Pompey. Livy's great work was a history of the Roman people; and in his preface he says that it will be reward enough for his labor in writing it if he can only forget for a while the troubles of his own times. This sounds rather mournful, but the history is charming. In reading it we almost feel that we are listening to Livy himself, for he writes his stories of the olden times as if he were telling them to a group of friends. He describes something that pleases him as if he

SCROLLS, WRITING UTENSILS, AND BOOKCASE
(Relief from a Roman Sarcophagus)

were sure that his readers would enjoy it with him; and he is as grieved over a lost battle of a century earlier as if the defeated general were his own dear friend.

Even when Ovid, or Publius O-vid'i-us Na'so, was a small boy, he was eager to write poetry. His father wished him to become an orator and win some high position in the government, and the boy tried his best to learn to argue. His teacher said that he spoke in a poetical sort of prose and did not arrange his arguments well. After a while a fortune was left him, and then he was free to write as much poetry as he chose. He was liked by the emperor, and life moved on most pleasantly. He wrote the *Met-a-mor'pho-ses*, or stories of the gods. One is the tale of the visit of Jupiter and Mercury to Bau'-cis and Phi-le'mon. It is so simply and naturally told that we can almost see old Baucis building a fire on the hearth, putting a piece of a broken dish under one leg of the table so it will stand even, then rubbing the board with mint to make it smell sweet. Ovid was revising his manuscript one even-

OVID
(From a Marble Statue by Ferrari)

THE REIGN OF AUGUSTUS

ing when an order for his banishment to the mouth of the Danube suddenly arrived from the emperor. No one ever knew why this was done. Ovid was torn from his family and sent to spend the rest of his life among the barbarians. In his despair he burned the *Metamorphoses*, but fortunately his friends had made copies of it long before. He died in exile.

It is because these great writers lived in the times of Augustus that his reign is called the Golden, or Au-gus'tan, Age of Latin literature. The reign is also marked by the closing of the gates of the temple of Janus. In war times these were always open; and the Romans had carried on wars so constantly that the gates had been closed only twice in seven hundred years. While Augustus ruled, they were closed three times. It was during one of these times when the world was at peace that Jesus was born in Bethlehem.

AUGUSTUS AND HIS FRIENDS
Hiltensperger

SUMMARY

Octavianus, or Augustus, ruled apparently by the old laws, but gradually got possession of all power. He made little attempt to enlarge the empire, but aimed at making the most of what it included. He governed the provinces wisely; he entertained the people, and the state provided grain for the poor at half price or less. Augustus reared many temples. The homes of the wealthy were most luxurious. Boys studied Greek, reading, writing, arithmetic, literature, and often oratory.

The greatest of Roman authors, Virgil, Horace, Livy, and Ovid, lived in the reign of Augustus; therefore this period is known as the Golden Age of Latin literature. While Augustus ruled, the gates of Janus were closed three times. In one of these periods of peace, Christ was born.

SUGGESTIONS FOR WRITTEN WORK

Augustus tells what he plans to do for Rome.
Was it wise to sell grain to the poor at half price?
A visit to a Roman home.
A schoolday in Rome.

XIV

THE REST OF THE TWELVE CAESARS

AUGUSTUS had finally chosen his step-son Tiberius to succeed him. The senate requested him to accept the office, but Tiberius pretended to be unwilling. He said that with so many illustrious patriots in Rome, he hoped they would not throw

THE REST OF THE TWELVE CAESARS

the whole care and responsibility upon one. The senators did not dare to take him at his word, so they wept and wailed and embraced his knees and begged him to become their emperor. He replied that he was not equal to the weight of the whole government, but that if they wished to intrust him with some special part, he would undertake it. One senator was unwise enough to ask what part he desired. Tiberius showed his anger at this so plainly that the frightened man hastened to say that he only asked in order to be convinced out of Tiberius's own mouth that the empire could not be divided, but must be governed by the mind of one person.

There were some legions of soldiers far away on the Rhine who were not afraid to say boldly that they did not want Tiberius for emperor, but their own commander, Ger-man'i-cus, a nephew of Tiberius. Germanicus was loyal. He made an earnest speech to his

TIBERIUS
(In the Lateran Museum, Rome)

soldiers and persuaded them to be true to Tiberius. He was at the place where Varus had suffered so terrible a defeat, and he succeeded in recovering one of the Roman eagles, the standards used in the army, which had been captured from

Varus. The Germans, however, were not subdued, but for some reason Tiberius recalled Germanicus and sent him to the East. He died of poison, given him, it is thought, at the command of the emperor.

For several years Tiberius seemed to be trying to govern his country well, but he was jealous of Germanicus, and after Germanicus was dead, he was suspicious of every one. Any act or word that could be reported as showing the least slight to the emperor was punished by death. The victim's property was confiscated, and the informer received a share. While Drusus, son of the emperor, was ill, a wealthy Roman wrote a poem about him. An informer asserted that to look forward to the death of one of the emperor's family and to think of a possible reward for a poem on the subject was deserving of the most severe punishment, and the poet was slain.

Tiberius was keen enough to see the falseness of his flatterers, and so suspicious that he trusted no one. Finally he left Rome altogether and went to the beautiful island of Ca'pre-æ (now called Capri) to spend the rest of his life. He chose a worthless man named Se-ja'nus to carry out his orders in Rome. Sejanus was so elated by this that he fancied he might become emperor if Tiberius's heirs were only dead. Therefore he poisoned Drusus and others; but at length he himself was put to death for plotting to murder the emperor.

At last Tiberius became so ill that his physician assured the court he could not live more than two days. All flocked about Ca-lig'u-la, son of Germanicus, for he was to be the next ruler, and each was eager to come first to congratulate him and so win his favor. Suddenly a message was brought, "Tiberius is much better and has called for food." The whole assembly trembled with fear, and Caligula expected nothing else than to be put to death; but the servants of Tiberius smothered the sick man. Thus his days ended.

It was while Tiberius was reigning that the crucifixion of Jesus took place in the far-away province of Judæa.

The senate now recognized as emperor Caligula, the son of Germanicus and grandnephew of Tiberius. His name was Caius Cæsar, but when he was a little boy, his mother took him to his father's camp dressed like a very small soldier. He wore *caligæ*, or half-boots with heavy nails, such as were worn by the common soldiers, and the men gave him the pet name of Caligula, or *little boot;* and even after he became emperor, he was always called by this nickname.

Caligula was half mad, and he had a wild reign. There was no limit to his insane freaks. One day he had a great crowd of people seized at random and thrown into the water because, as he said, he wanted to see something unusual. The gladiatorial contests became more savage than ever. When he longed to see more people slain, he sometimes drove the spectators into the arena with the wild beasts. He plundered Gaul and set sail for Britain, but turned back before he was fairly at sea and ordered his soldiers to pick up shells to carry to Rome. He declared his favorite horse to be a consul, and he used to invite it to his table and present it with gilt corn in a golden basin. Then the horse was led back to his golden manger in his ivory stable. Caligula meant to destroy the works of Ho'mer, Virgil, and Livy; and he meant to murder the greater part of the senate; but a conspiracy was formed against him and he was slain.

Caligula had been afraid of assassination, and to protect himself he had formed a bodyguard, or prætorian guard, as it was called, of six thousand soldiers. These soldiers had become very powerful, and when Caligula died, they declared that his uncle Claudius, the brother of Germanicus, should be their emperor. People had thought Claudius was almost an imbecile, and he had been wise enough to do nothing to prevent them from thinking so, that no one might consider it worth while to murder him. After he was made emperor, however, he was not afraid to be himself. He built for Rome an aqueduct and a most excellent harbor. He requested the senate to allow the nobles of Germany to become senators, and when they hesitated, he reminded them that Romulus admitted other tribes. "My own ancestor," he said, "was a Sabine, but he was received into Rome and made a patrician." The senate yielded.

Tiberius had threatened to invade Britain, and Claudius determined to conquer the island. He sent first a skilful general, and then he himself followed. Southern Britain was subdued, and the British chief Ca-rac'ta-cus was carried to Rome as a captive. The Romans looked upon him as a savage barbarian, but he was calm and dignified, and when there was opportunity for him to speak to the emperor, he declared that he, too, was a prince and was descended from illustrious ancestors. "I had men and arms, horses, and riches," he said, "and where is the wonder if I was unwilling to part with them? If you Romans aim at ruling all man-

THE REST OF THE TWELVE CAESARS 187

kind, it does not follow that all men should take the yoke upon them." In some way Claudius was persuaded to set him and his family free. They bowed in gratitude before him, then before his wife Ag-rip-pi'na, who sat on a throne near that of the emperor. She had married him in order that her son Ne'ro by a former husband might succeed him. He had yielded to her will and had adopted Nero, but Agrip-

NERO AFTER THE BURNING OF ROME

pina became tired of waiting for her husband to die, and she poisoned him.

Nero became emperor at the age of seventeen. In spite of the wickedness of his mother, he had been carefully trained, for the writer Sen'e-ca had been his teacher. Seneca tried his best to make him kind and good. "Life is short, therefore live peaceably with all men," he said. "Live so that all will love you, and then they will mourn for you when you die." For a few years Nero obeyed him. This did not please Agrippina, and she threatened to induce the soldiers to make Nero's half-brother emperor. Then Nero slew both the half-brother and his mother. When he had been reigning ten years, a fire broke out in Rome which swept away the greater part of the city. Nero did all that he could to help the people who had lost everything. He put up buildings for them, threw open his gardens that they might have a refuge, and ordered grain to be sold at an extremely low price. Nevertheless, it was said that he had kindled the fire and had played on his lyre and sung while it was burning. Whether this was true or not, Nero was frightened and looked about him for some one to blame.

The religion of Christ had been preached in Rome, and there were many Christians in the city. The Romans could not understand a worship without images or temples, and they looked upon the followers of Jesus as heathen. The Christians believed it wrong to join in the worship of the gods and in the Roman festivals in their honor, and therefore the Romans called them, "Men who hate their fellow-men." It had become a custom to worship the emperor as a god and to burn incense before his statue. Christians could not take part in this, and therefore the Romans said they were not loyal, and if any misfortune came upon the state, it was often laid to their neglect of what was due to the gods. Nero laid

THE REST OF THE TWELVE CAESARS

the burning of the city to them and put large numbers of them to death. Some he crucified; some he covered with the skins of wild beasts and then set savage dogs upon them; some he smeared with pitch and burned at night to light his gardens. Even the angry and suffering Romans pitied them.

After the fire the city was rebuilt. Money and treasures and statues of the gods were taken from the temples or wherever they could be found, whether in the provinces or in Italy itself, and brought to Rome to beautify the new city. Nero built himself a magnificent house with a portico a mile long. Its vestibule was lofty enough to give room to a statue of the emperor

THE ROMAN FORUM IN THE TIME OF NERO

one hundred and twenty feet high. His banqueting room had pipes by which perfumes might be showered over the guests, and the ceiling was so curiously made that at a touch flowers were scattered among them. Everything was crusted with gems and mother-of-pearl. Around the house stretched vineyards and woods and fields and pools so beautifully laid out and giving such extensive views that the historian Tac′i-tus declared they were more wonderful than the buildings. Nero called his dwelling his Golden House. When it was finished, he boasted that at last he had a home that was fit for a man to live in.

Nero grew worse and worse — if a man as bad as he could grow any worse. Plots were formed against him, and he put Seneca to death on the charge of having joined in one of them. The armies in the provinces revolted, the prætorian guard refused to protect him, and finally the senate decreed that he should be scourged to death. When he heard of this, he took his own life.

HEAD OF NERO
(In the Capitoline Museum, Rome)

Who should be made emperor? There were no more of the family of Cæsar, and any one who had influence enough might hope to win the prize. The troops in Spain declared that Gal′ba, their general, should rule, and the senate thought it wise to agree with them. But in Rome there was one O′tho who was a favorite with the prætorian guard. He hoped to be adopted by Galba and to succeed him. Galba adopted some one else; then the guard killed him and proclaimed Otho emperor. This was satisfactory to the army in the East; but the army in Gaul and Spain declared that their general Vi-tel′li-us should become emperor. Part of Vitellius's army were on

THE REST OF THE TWELVE CAESARS 191

their way back to Italy. They met Otho and defeated him, and he took his own life. Vitellius was then in power; but there was also an army in Syria to be pleased. They claimed the throne for their general, Ves-pa'si-an, and at length Vitellius was put to death and Vespasian was made emperor.

Vespasian was an honest old soldier who meant to do his best for the Romans. He had no easy position, for Rome was in disorder, there was a revolt in the region of the Rhine, and there was war in Judæa. He set to work first to make Rome orderly. He paid sincere respect to the senate, he lived simply and reasonably, and he saw to it that the laws were obeyed. He suppressed the revolt of the Gauls. The war in Judæa he left for his son Titus to carry on. Titus besieged Jerusalem. Though the Jews fought to the last to defend their temple and the Holy City, the Romans

JERUSALEM TAKEN BY TITUS

were victorious. The Jewish historian Jo-se'phus had fought Vespasian boldly, but had returned to Rome with him and received pardon. He went back to Jerusalem and tried his best to persuade his countrymen to surrender, but they would not. Afterward he wrote an account of the sufferings of the people and the capture of the city which is almost too terrible to read. The wonderful temple, its front covered with plates of gold of amazing weight and of such brilliancy that no one could look at it when the light shone upon it at sunrise, fell into the hands of the Romans. They took what they would, then set to work to destroy the city. Three towers were left to show the strength of the fortifications that the Romans had demolished, then all that remained was so completely overthrown that, as Josephus wrote, no one would have known it had ever been inhabited. It is thought that one million of Jews perished. Those that were left were scattered through many countries.

The soldier emperor had a care also for the things of the mind. The famous Quin-til'i-an taught rhetoric and oratory in Rome, and Vespasian was so pleased with his teaching that he gave him a salary from the imperial treasury. Quintilian had a little son whom he dearly loved, and his best work is a book about oratory which he composed for the boy to read when he should be old enough. The child died, and Quintilian wrote piteously, "What shall I do? I have lost the only comfort of my declining years."

In the tumults before Vespasian was firmly seated upon the throne, the temple on the Capitoline Hill had been destroyed. He rebuilt it, and also a new forum. He began the gathered. The vast arena could be flooded by underground pipes almost in an instant, and thus afford an excellent opportunity for displays of mock naval battles. There were sixty or eighty ascending rows of seats made of marble and richly cushioned. A canopy gave protection from the sun and the rain. In this building the people of Rome sat and watched the bloody death of thousands of men and wild beasts.

The Romans were so used to bloodshed that they seem to have seldom felt compassion for suffering. Titus grieved that he had "lost a day" when during its hours he had done no one a kindness, and he was so good and just and generous that his people called him "the delight of mankind"; but even he was so hardened to suffering that after the fall of Jerusalem he had twenty-five hundred Jews burned to death or slain in contests with wild

DESTRUCTION OF POMPEII

beasts or with one another — and this was in honor of his brother Do-mi'ti-an's birthday!

During the reign of Titus, a second great fire swept over Rome. There was, too, a terrible eruption of Mount Vesuvius which buried the cities of Her-cu-la'ne-um and Pom-pe'i-i. The elder Plin'y, a famous author, lost his life in this eruption; his nephew, who is spoken of as the younger Pliny, was a young man of eighteen at the time of the disaster. He wrote to the historian Tacitus a long letter about the awful calamity. He believed that the end of all things had come and that he was "perishing with the world itself."

ARCH OF TITUS

Titus was succeeded by his brother Domitian. During the reign of the latter, his general A-gric'o-la conquered Britain far into what is now Scotland, and built a wall from the Forth to the Clyde to keep off the savage tribes of the north. He planned to conquer Ireland; but Domitian had become jealous of his successful general and recalled him. The Da'ci-ans, who lived along the Danube, revolted, and Domitian himself went forth to quiet them. It was said that he never met the enemy, and that his forces were worsted in several engagements. Nevertheless, he returned to Rome in great glory and gave himself a triumph. He had no real captives to walk in the procession, for the excellent reason that he had not succeeded in taking any; but he bought large numbers of slaves and dressed them to represent the people whom he had failed to conquer. To free Rome from the attacks of these tribes, he humbled himself to give them every year a certain weight of gold. Pliny the younger declared that whenever Domitian celebrated a triumph, the Romans might be sure that not they, but their enemies, had gained something. Domitian drove away from the city all the literary men and philosophers. One of the most interest-

DOMITIAN
(In the Vatican)

ing of the latter was Ep-ic-te'tus. He was born a slave, but had become free by some means. He lived in a little hut, which was furnished with a bed and a lamp and nothing more; but he spoke so wisely about matters of life and thought that people were always eager to listen to him. His favorite maxim was, "Bear and forbear."

Domitian governed the provinces firmly and wisely. He enforced the religious observances of the state and punished severely those who violated them. At the death of an emperor, it had become the custom among the Romans to declare that he had joined the gods and to offer up prayers to him. Domitian had no idea of waiting for these honors until he was dead. He set up statues of himself and commanded his subjects to burn incense before them. This, of course, neither the Jews nor the Christians could do; and therefore he persecuted them savagely. It was at this time that the apostle John was banished to the island of Pat'mos.

Early in Domitian's reign, part of his army and many senators conspired against him, and from that time he was suspicious of everyone and put many to death because of his fears. At last he was assassinated. It is said that his own wife joined in the plot against him. The senate decreed that his name should be struck out of their annals and erased from the various monuments.

These emperors, Julius, Augustus, Tiberius, Caligula, Claudius, Nero, Galba, Otho, Vitellius, Vespasian, Titus, and Domitian, are often spoken of as the "Twelve Cæsars," but for no better reason than that the historian Sue-to'ni-us, a friend of Pliny's, wrote the biographies of these twelve and

THE REST OF THE TWELVE CAESARS

no more. "Cæsar" had come to be regarded as a title rather than a family name, and signified "emperor" or "sovereign." Of these twelve, only three, Augustus, Vespasian, and perhaps Titus, died a natural death; and only one, Vespasian, was succeeded by his own son.

SUMMARY

Tiberius became emperor, though the soldiers on the Rhine wanted Germanicus. Tiberius was jealous and suspicious. He withdrew to Capreæ. During the reign of Tiberius, Christ was crucified. At the death of Tiberius, Caligula became emperor. He was a strange, wild ruler. Caligula formed the prætorian guard. At his death, they demanded Claudius for their emperor. Claudius allowed the German nobles to become senators. He began the conquest of Britain.

Nero was accused of setting fire to Rome. He persecuted the Christians. The city was rebuilt and beautified. Nero's home was called the Golden House. In fear, he took his own life. Galba, Otho, Vitellius, and Vespasian became emperor successively. During the reign of Vespasian, his son Titus captured Jerusalem. Vespasian favored the orator Quintilian; he began the Colosseum and reared other structures. Titus built elaborate bathhouses and completed the Colosseum. While Titus reigned, Herculaneum and Pompeii were destroyed, in 79 A.D.

Domitian bribed the Dacians to leave Rome in peace. He banished Epictetus and other philosophers and literary men. He recalled Agricola from Britain. He persecuted the Christians and banished St. John to Patmos. "Cæsar" was now regarded as a title rather than a family name.

SUGGESTIONS FOR WRITTEN WORK

Caligula tells of his visit to his father's camp.
What Caractacus thought of the Romans.
What Juvenal thought of the Romans.
An hour in the Golden House.

XV

THE FIVE GOOD EMPERORS

THE rule of the "Twelve Cæsars" extended over nearly one hundred and fifty years. During the greater part of this time, the provinces suffered little from the cruelty of the emperors, but the history of the city is one long story of tyranny and bloodshed. It is a relief to read that these Twelve were followed by honest, faithful men, the "Five Good Emperors," who did all that they could for the best good of the empire.

The first of these five rulers was Ner'va, a kind-hearted, elderly man. He recalled those who had been exiled; he lessened the taxes of the people; and he put an end to the wretched business of the informers, who were always on the watch to report the utterance of a word against the emperor. Indeed, he was so gentle and forgiving that one senator said, "It is ill to have a prince under whom no one may do anything; but worse to have one who lets everyone do as he will." The murderers of Domitian had not been punished, and now the prætorian guard took the matter into their own hands and put to death without a trial as many of them as

THE FIVE GOOD EMPERORS

could be found. Nerva was not able to punish this rebellion against his authority, and he decided to adopt an energetic young general of Spanish birth named Tra'jan, and let him share in the government. A few months later Nerva died.

Trajan was near the Rhine with the army when it was announced to him that he had become emperor. He went on fortifying the frontier, and a year passed before he appeared in Rome. Then he walked quietly and without guards to the palace of the Cæsars.

Trajan proved to be an ideal emperor in the eyes of the Romans, and they gave him the title of *Op'-ti-mus*, or *best*. He scorned the thought of paying tribute to the Dacians, as Domitian had done. He suppressed them; and in remembrance of his victories he laid out a new forum with one library for Latin books and another for Greek, a magnificent basilica, statues, and a triumphal arch. In the centre of this forum he placed a column about which wound a band of sculpture

TRAJAN

telling the story of the Dacian War. At the summit of the column was the statue of the emperor himself.

Trajan did not agree with Augustus that the empire was large enough. He carried on war in the East and made large conquests to the southeast of the Black Sea.

Under this vigorous ruler, baths, theatres, and other handsome structures were built not only in Rome, but scattered through the provinces. He looked out for the roads and

COLUMN AND FORUM OF TRAJAN

bridges; he made arrangements for caring for poor children; and he loaned money at less than half the usual rates to landowners who wished to improve their property.

This many-sided emperor enjoyed being with literary men. Pliny the Younger, who wrote the account of the eruption of Mount Vesuvius, was one of his correspondents. Plutarch,

THE FIVE GOOD EMPERORS

too, lived during the reign, and wrote his "Lives," the biographies of forty-six Greeks and Romans, told so simply and naturally and with so many anecdotes that every generation since they were written has found them well worth reading.

The Romans would have been glad if Trajan had left a son to rule them as well as he had done. After his death his wife announced that in his illness he had adopted a young relative, named Ha'dri-an, and he became emperor.

Hadrian believed that the empire was as large as could be well managed, and he even gave up some of the lands overpowered by Trajan in the East. Then he set out to become acquainted with every corner of his realm, and, followed by his legions, he traveled from one country to another. Sometimes he rode on horseback, but far oftener he marched with his soldiers. He drilled them severely, but he took care for their rights; and whatever came to them as rations, cheese, bread, and sour wine, he always tasted for himself. On through Gaul he journeyed, then to Britain. There he found a flourishing province with plenty of grain for home use and for export, with potteries, roads, cities, handsome villas, and elaborate baths. He built a wall south of Agricola's, running from near the mouth of the Tyne River to Solway Firth, close to what is now the dividing line between England and Scotland. On this wall there were watchtowers, and at intervals of every four miles a fort. Leaving Britain, Hadrian passed southward through Gaul again, then visited Spain, northern Africa, the countries beyond the Ti'gris and Euphra'tes rivers, Athens, Carthage, and so back to Rome. He had gone to Athens when a boy of ten and had spent five years there in study. He must have had pleasant recollections of the city, for he seemed eager to do something for it. In other places on his way he had erected public buildings, temples, and theatres; but in Athens he not only reared many of these, but completed a superb temple to Jupiter, begun long before, which became wonderfully beautiful with his lavish gifts of statues, paintings, and decorations of gold and ivory. He also erected a famous arch which is still standing.

ARCH OF HADRIAN, ATHENS

The greater part of fifteen years Hadrian spent in journeying about his empire. Before his time the provincials had been obliged to provide post-wagons free

THE FIVE GOOD EMPERORS

for the use of the government; but Hadrian saw how heavy a burden this was, and he paid his own traveling expenses.

The founding of a colony on the former site of Jerusalem aroused the Jews to make a desperate struggle against their conquerors. After they were subdued, he forbade their entering the city save on one day in each year, the anniversary of its overthrow.

Hadrian spent his last years in Rome, or at a splendid villa which he had built a few miles outside the city. He built also temples and a vast mausoleum for his own tomb. This was a round building faced with white marble, and encircled by rows of pillars and statues. It is now known as the Castle of Saint Angelo. He adopted as his son and successor a Gaul named An-to-ni'nus, and bade him adopt Marcus Au-re'li-us, a young man of seventeen, and also a little boy, Lucius Ve'rus, who was ten years younger. Antoninus was so respectful to the memory of Hadrian that the Romans gave him the title of *Pi'us*, that is, *the duti-*

HADRIAN'S TOMB
(Now called Castle of St. Angelo)

ful; and he is known in history as Antoninus Pius. For twenty-three years he reigned, or rather he and the young Marcus Aurelius reigned together. He was kind and dignified as a private citizen; and he did not change when he became emperor. His one care seemed to be how to secure the best good of his subjects.

At the death of Antoninus Pius, Marcus Aurelius Antoninus became emperor. He shared his rule with Verus until the death of the latter. For nineteen years he reigned, and the greater part of the time, this student who would have been so glad to spend the years in reading and thinking was obliged to spend them at the head of the army. The barbarians along the frontiers of the empire were pushed upon by other barbarians beyond them, and they were pressing toward Italy. The soldiers returning from the East brought pestilence with them. The land was filled with sickness and the treasury was low. There was no strength to subdue the barbarians; the most that could be done was to try to check their advance. From one part of the frontier to another the weary emperor went, always planning how to protect his

ANTONINUS PIUS

realm and how to rule it well. He was a student of Epictetus, and he himself was a philosopher. When he had a moment of leisure, he often occupied it in writing thoughts that would help him to keep good and true in the troubles that thronged about him. When he was in camp near the Danube, he found a few minutes to write how much he had learned from Antoninus Pius, how much from each of those who taught him as a boy, and in how many things he found himself singularly fortunate. He wrote many wise and sensible thoughts like the following: —

MARCUS AURELIUS

"What is not good for the swarm is not good for the bee.

"Consider how much more pain is brought on us by the anger and vexation caused by such acts than by the acts themselves at which we are angry and vexed.

"The best way of avenging yourself is not to become like the wrongdoer."

Through the reign of the Five Good Emperors, eighty-four years, there had been good government in Rome; but if earnest, faithful Marcus Aurelius could have looked forward a few years, he might well have feared for the future of the empire.

SUMMARY

The "Twelve Cæsars" were followed by the "Five Good Emperors." The first of the five was Nerva, who was upright and kind, but not strong enough to rule. Trajan was called Optimus by his people. He suppressed the Dacians, erected buildings, and conquered the lands lying southeast of the Black Sea. Among his literary friends were Pliny the Younger and Plutarch. Hadrian traveled over his realm. In Britain, he built the wall called by his name. Elsewhere he reared handsome buildings, particularly in Athens. He suppressed a revolt of Jews and forbade their entering Jerusalem.

After Trajan came Antoninus Pius, and then Marcus Aurelius Antoninus. The latter was a student and philosopher.

SUGGESTIONS FOR WRITTEN WORK

Two persons talk together of Nerva and Trajan.

Hadrian talks of his visit to Britain.

Which do you think is the best of the three sayings quoted from Marcus Aurelius? Why?

XVI

FROM MARCUS AURELIUS TO DIOCLETIAN

So wise a man as Marcus Aurelius must have seen that there were several reasons why the empire was not so strong as it had been in the earlier times. In the first place, there was a lack of citizens. Vast numbers had been slain in the wars, and the custom of casting infants out to perish had become so common that the places of these men had not been filled. Then, too, there was no stable government. If an emperor respected the senate, he deferred to its wishes; if not, he went very much his own way. It is hard to feel devotion to a country with an unstable government, and patriotism had almost disappeared.

Again, the Romans scorned work; and slaves had been so cheap that work had been left to them while the masters lived in idleness. Land was in the hands of the few rather than the many. Grain could be brought to Italy cheaper than it could be raised there, and the small farmers had gradually given up their farms and joined the crowds of idle folk in the city, doing no work, and depending upon the government for food and amusement. Everyone wanted luxuries, such as silks and spices; and they must be brought from the East. The chief manufactures of the Mediterranean countries were leather and wool, and the East did not care for these. In consequence, Rome had to pay in silver or gold for all her Eastern imports. Therefore, the silver and gold were going out of the country rapidly. More did not come in, for the wealth of Rome had come not from production, but from conquest, and now the conquests had ceased.

Taxes were high; there was no definite arrangement by which when one emperor died, the people could be sure who would succeed him. The conquered nations had small interest in Rome, and from the Romans themselves they had learned how to wage war to the death when they wished to rebel. Moreover, beyond this ring of conquered nations there were hordes of barbarians crowding nearer and nearer to the Roman boundaries, and the best strength of the empire was constantly called upon to check their advance. If there was a fire, a famine, or an earthquake with loss of people and property, there was no way to make the loss good.

A long succession of strong, wise rulers might have done much to make the empire strong and united; but the first one to follow the good Marcus Aurelius was his son Com'mo-dus, and a more unworthy son of a worthy man never lived. His chief pleasure was gladiatorial contests; and he was not satisfied with seeing bloodshed, he must cause it with his own weapons. More than seven hundred times the emperor of Rome degraded himself by entering the arena and contending with wild beasts, or with men armed with weapons of lead or tin. The senate meekly bestowed upon him various titles of honor, but the one that pleased him most was the "Roman Hercules."

He was followed by Per'ti-nax, who would gladly have brought about many reforms; but the prætorians did not wish a ruler of that stamp, and they actually auctioned off the Roman empire. One wealthy man offered eight hundred dollars to each soldier of the guard; but a second offered a thousand dollars, and it was knocked down to him. Each of the armies in other parts of the realm declared its own general to be emperor. The strongest of all these candidates was Lucius Sep-tim'i-us Se-ve'rus. He won the prize, and the purchaser of the empire was slain.

Much of the reign of Severus was spent in trying to thrust the barbarians back from the frontier. The deed by which he is most clearly remembered is his disbanding of the old prætorian guard of Italians and forming another. This new guard consisted of fifty thousand men, and they were of all nationalities. The chief power was held by these foreign soldiers; and therefore Rome was already in the hands of strangers, though no one realized it. A man might do whatever he chose if only he could win over the soldiers. It was easy to win them if one had gold enough, and taxing the people would bring in gold. The emperor Car-a-cal'la, son of Severus, was so in need of money for this purpose that to increase the taxes he admitted to citizenship all freeborn people throughout the empire.

Of the many men who sat on the imperial throne between 180 A. D. and 268 A. D., few are worthy of notice. One was a young boy from Syria; one an ignorant peasant; at one time there were actually thirty generals, the Thirty Tyrants, as they are called, each of whom claimed the right to rule. The soldiers put anyone in power who had made them gifts or whom they fancied for the moment; and when they were tired of him, they murdered him and put in some one else. The better an emperor was, the sooner he was put to death.

Alexander Severus did all that a man could do to control the soldiers and rule the country well; but of course in such a condition his reign was short.

Matters began to look darker and darker. The army was the only power in the empire. A soldier's first duty is to obey; and as this army had no idea of obeying anything but their own will, they were not valuable soldiers. Unfortunately for Rome, her enemies grew strong as her soldiers grew weak, and the Romans were defeated in battle after battle. Rome never needed loyal defenders worse, for the Germans on the Rhine and the Danube were pushing into the Roman lands; and Persia, on the east, had become a powerful kingdom. In Rome itself there was no government at all, for no one could hope to become emperor who was not a general of one army or another, and no army would recognize any general but its own. The whole empire was in confusion. It did not seem as if order could be restored for

RUINS AT PALMYRA
(Colonnade and Triumphal Arch)

even a moment; but it came about that once more five good men in succession held the throne and ruled so wisely and with so strong a hand that for a few years the fate of the empire seemed more hopeful.

Au-re′li-an, one of these five, made the famous capture of Pal-my′ra. This was a wealthy city on an oasis in the Syrian desert. Its ruler was Ze-no′bi-a, a woman who was every inch a queen. She was finely educated; she could ride or walk at the head of the troops; and she could command them. It was said that several of her husband's victories were due to her excellent

THE APPIAN WAY
(As it looked during the Empire)

generalship. Some of these victories had been won over the Persian king, and the Romans had shown much gratitude. At her husband's death, she took the throne. The Romans objected and sent an army against her, which she promptly defeated. It was thought that she was planning an empire that should rival Rome, and Aurelian himself took up arms to overthrow Palmyra. He wrote home, "The Roman people speak with contempt of the war which I am waging against a woman. They are ignorant both of the character and of the power of Zenobia." After a siege Palmyra surrendered and was destroyed. Zenobia was captured and taken to Rome. There she was sumptuously dressed, bound with golden fetters, and loaded with glittering jewels of many colors. About her neck was wound a golden chain so heavy that a slave had to help her carry it; and in these trappings she walked through the streets of Rome in the triumph of Aurelian. After this, Aurelian gave her a handsome residence twenty miles from the city, and there she and her children lived.

The end of the reign of the five emperors came in the year 284 A.D. The throne fell next to Di-o-cle'ti-an, who made so many changes that he seemed almost the "founder of a new empire."

SUMMARY

The empire was becoming weak from loss of citizens, lack of stable government, idleness, love of luxury, and cessation of conquests. Marcus Aurelius was followed by his gladiator son Commodus. The empire was sold at auction. Severus formed a new prætorian guard of foreign soldiers. Caracalla admitted to citizenship all freeborn people in the empire. The soldiers made emperor whomever they chose. The empire was in confusion. Aurelian captured and destroyed Palmyra in 273 A.D.

SUGGESTIONS FOR WRITTEN WORK

A Roman tells why the empire is becoming weak.
Why was it an especial shame for an emperor to be a gladiator?
Why was it unwise to admit all freeborn people to citizenship?

XVII

REIGNS OF DIOCLETIAN AND CONSTANTINE

No one who thought for a moment about the state of the empire could have helped seeing that remedies must be found at once for at least two of its troubles. In the first place, the lives of the emperors must be protected so they should not be slain at the whim of the soldiers. Second, the barbarians who were pressing upon the boundaries must be thrust back. Diocletian saw this, and discovered, or thought he had discovered a certain remedy. Whether certain or not, it was surely an original one. He chose three generals to aid him in the government. To one of these he gave the title of *Augustus*, which he himself bore. The other two were called *Cæsars*. His plan was that the four should work together, each ruling a division of the empire. When an Augustus died, a Cæsar was to be promoted to take his place and another Cæsar to be chosen.

There were three reasons why this arrangement seemed to Diocletian a most excellent plan. One was that the succession to the throne was provided for. The second was that the four men could divide the realm among them, and so it would be well cared for and protected. The third was that it would prevent assassination, for the murder of one or two or even three of the four would not change the government in the least; and it would not be easy to plot to kill four men in different parts of the vast empire at the same moment.

All went on smoothly for a while, but it was soon found that keeping up four courts and four sets of officials was an expensive matter. Diocletian had taken Egypt, Asia, and Thrace for his share, and had chosen Nic-o-me′di-a, near the Bos′pho-rus, as his capital. Here he lived in the utmost luxury and splendor. The emperor Augustus had gone about among the people in familiar fashion, had lived simply, and had dressed like other well-to-do Romans. The emperor Diocletian dressed in robes of silk and gold and even ornamented his shoes with the most precious gems. Instead of the people's meeting their emperor easily and familiarly, there were numerous officials to be passed before anyone could reach the presence chamber. There the visitor was required to throw himself upon the ground at the feet of the ruler. Moreover, this ruler wore a crown, a thing which neither Julius nor Augustus would have ventured to do. Augustus had kept up all the old forms of the republic and had done his best to make the people feel that they were the real rulers, and he was only one of themselves. Diocletian dropped the old forms and did everything to remove himself from the people and induce them to feel that he was not a mere man, but a creature far above them and of finer clay than they.

To keep up this expensive court, and those of the other

DIOCLETIAN AND CONSTANTINE 217

rulers, required money, as has been said before, and money must be obtained by increasing the taxes of the people. These taxes were already severe, and soon there was rebellion on the part of the peasants in Gaul. These peasants were subdued by arms, but they felt that they were burdened beyond what was just and right, and they were angry and discontented.

Diocletian was inclined to permit the Christians to carry on their worship as they would, but Ga-le'ri-us, one of the Cæsars, was strongly opposed to them. At length Diocletian

CHRISTIAN MARTYRS IN THE COLOSSEUM

yielded to him and passed severe laws against them. Their churches were leveled to the ground, and they themselves were tortured, thrown to wild beasts in the arena, or put to death in other ways.

While this persecution was still going on, the Roman world was amazed to learn that both Diocletian and Max-im′i-an, the second Augustus, had given up the throne and intended to spend the rest of their lives as private citizens. Diocletian withdrew to Dal-ma′ti-a, and there on the shore of the Adriatic Sea he built himself a palace. Maximian soon regretted his abdication and wrote to Diocletian to ask if they could not by working together get possession of the sovereignty again. Diocletian gave him little comfort, for he replied, "Were you but to come to Sa-lo′na and see the vegetables which I raise in my garden with my own hands, you would no longer talk to me of empire."

The persecution of the Christians continued for seven years after the retirement of Diocletian. Galerius finally published an edict putting an end to it. He was then in his last sickness, and it is said that in his sufferings he besought the Christians to pray to their God for him.

When Diocletian and Maximian gave up the throne, Galerius and Con-stan′ti-us became Augusti. So far the plan of Diocletian had worked smoothly; but when Constantius died, the soldiers put aside all Diocletian's plans and declared that their commander, Con-stan-ti′nus, or Con′-stan-tine, should be emperor. There were, however, several other claimants to the throne, of whom the most active was Max-en′ti-us. It was several years, therefore, before Constantine became the undisputed ruler of the empire.

Instead of persecuting the Christians, Constantine took the cross for his standard. He declared that one day at noon, during his struggle with his rival, Maxentius, he saw a cross

DIOCLETIAN AND CONSTANTINE

THE VISION OF CONSTANTINE
(From a Painting in the Vatican)

in the sky above the sun, and on it was written, in Greek, *In this sign thou shalt conquer*, or, as it was translated into Latin, *In hoc signo vinces*. On the following day, he displayed a cross to his soldiers. From its shorter beam hung a banner of purple silk, flashing with jewels and showing images of him and his children. On the top of the upright beam was a golden crown marked ☧, the Greek letters which stand for the cross and also for the *Ch-r* of "Christ." On this day he fought with Maxentius the battle of Mil'vi-an Bridge, one of his most important engagements, and won a great victory. Henceforth his army followed the cross in all their battles. One year later, Constantine published an edict (the Edict of Mil'an) allowing everyone in his realm to practice whatever religion he might choose. Little by little he gave the Christians more rights. Their numbers increased rapidly, for few people had now any faith in the gods, and they had suffered so much that they were glad to learn of a God in whom they could believe.

So it was that the empire gained a new faith. It was not long before it gained a new capital, for Constantine decided to take By-zan'ti-um on the Bosphorus for his chief city. He was a wise man, and he had several good reasons for doing this. Perhaps the strongest of all was that he meant to rule the empire without paying any attention to the Roman senate or the nobles; and this would be much easier to do in the East where people had always been accustomed to bowing down to their rulers. Another reason was that in Byzantium the emperor would be nearer his most dangerous enemies, the barbarians north of the Danube and the Persians. He would also be nearer the mass of his people. Now that Rome ruled Greece and Asia Minor, Byzantium was in a most excellent location for carrying on trade, since all the commerce of the countries around the Black Sea must pass through the Bosphorus. The new city was given the name of Con-stan-ti-no'ple, or city of Constantine. It is said that more than twelve million dollars was spent on walls, porticoes, and aqueducts alone. Baths, theatres, forum, circus, churches, palaces, all sprang up within a short time. The city was adorned with the works of the greatest artists, for the builder was the master of the world, and he took from the cities of Greece and Asia Minor the finest statues and most perfect ornaments that were in existence.

ARCH OF CONSTANTINE
(Built in Commemoration of the Victory at Milvian Bridge)

The next thing to do was to make the government as strong as possible, or rather, to prevent anyone's interfering with what Constantine thought best to do, for he himself proposed to be the government. He had decided that the surest way to prevent revolts was not to allow any one man to have too much power. Therefore he made many generals and gave each one fewer soldiers than had been the custom; and he divided the provinces into small districts. This way of ruling prevented rebellions, but it was expensive, for there were very many officials to be paid, and therefore the taxes of the people rose still higher. Those who had fertile lands far enough from the frontiers to be well protected could generally pay what was demanded; but men near the boundaries whose fields were sometimes devastated by barbarians could not pay, and gradually they abandoned their lands. The result of this was that after a while the country at a safe distance from the boundaries was cultivated; but that which was near the borders of the empire was left wild.

After Constantine's death, first his sons and then his nephew ruled the empire. This nephew was Ju'li-an. He is called "the Apostate," because he gave up Christianity and tried to bring his people back to the worship of the old gods. The days of the persecutions had passed, but Julian gave the chief offices to those who would carry on the old worship. He forbade Christians to teach in the schools, and he made them rebuild the temples that had been ruined. He made several campaigns against the Persians, and in one of these he was fatally wounded. His successor was a Christian. With Julian died the last imperial worshipper of the gods.

SUMMARY

It had become necessary to protect the emperor and keep back the barbarians. Diocletian shared his power with three others. This was very expensive, and the increase of taxes resulted in rebellion. The Christians were persecuted. Diocletian and Maximian abdicated. At the death of the Augusti, the soldiers made Constantine emperor. His vision of the cross and his success at Milvian Bridge led him to take the cross for his standard. He granted religious freedom. Byzantium, or Constantinople, became the capital and was most richly adorned. To prevent rebellions, Constantine divided the army and the provinces into small districts. Taxes were increased, and land near the boundaries was abandoned. Julian the Apostate tried to restore the worship of the gods.

SUGGESTIONS FOR WRITTEN WORK

What a Roman thought of Diocletian's division of the imperial power.

A visit to the emperor Diocletian.

Diocletian writes to Maximian about the pleasures of his life in the country.

XVIII

THE LAST CENTURIES OF THE EMPIRE

THE Persians were determined enemies, but Rome had far more powerful ones to meet, and these were the Germans, who have already been mentioned several times. They were a wild, barbarous people, divided into many different tribes. They lived beyond the Rhine and the Danube. They were tall and large. They had light hair and keen, fierce blue eyes. They were brave and strong, and they only laughed at cold and weariness. They wore the skins of wild beasts and sometimes a coarse sort of linen, or else the gorgeous garments which they had captured or bought of the provincials.

These were the people who had attacked Rome even in the days when it was a republic. Marius defeated the German Cimbri and Teutones in 102 B. C., and ever since then the Romans had been continually driving away one tribe or another of them. For many years the empire had been growing weaker, and all this time the Germans had been growing stronger and bolder, and they never left the Romans in peace. Sometimes a few of them stole into the Roman domains and drove off some cattle. Sometimes they came in larger numbers and destroyed houses and crops throughout a whole province. Sometimes they came peacefully and with the emperor's permission and made settlements on Roman lands. Sometimes they became allies of the Romans.

As time passed, they learned much of the ways of the Romans, not only their methods of warfare, but also their customs of living. Wild and rude as the Germans were, they had an exceedingly fine trait, — they were anxious to learn, and when they discovered a better way of doing anything than their own, they were eager to adopt it. The more these barbarians saw and heard of Italy, the more they were charmed by that warm, sunny country, and by the rich, splendid life of the Romans. It is no wonder that they were determined, whether by fair means or foul, to break into the empire. Those of the German tribes that succeeded in doing this became devoted to their adopted country. Many of them joined the Roman legions and were as anxious as any of the Romans to save the land from its enemies, — even from the barbarians of their own race.

In the fourth century, a tribe of Germans called Vis'i-goths, or Western Goths, lived to the north just beyond the Danube. They came to the Romans in great distress. "A fearful people, the Huns, are upon us," they said, "and we cannot resist them. Only let us cross the Danube. Grant us homes in

Thrace, and we will obey the Roman laws and guard the empire from the horrible savages."

It was difficult to decide what reply to make to this petition. If the answer was "No," the Visigoths might come, nevertheless, in vast numbers and as enemies rather than suppliants. On the other hand, to allow hundreds of thousands of armed men to cross the boundary river was a dangerous thing to do. Va'lens, emperor in the East (for the empire was now divided, and there was one emperor in the East and another in the West), made the blunder of trying to do things by halves. He told the Goths that they might come and that he would provide food; but they must surrender their weapons and give up the children of their chief men as hostages. They agreed to this. Next came the passing of the river. It was no easy matter, for there were nearly a million of the Goths; but at length it was completed. The children of the leaders were carried to distant parts of the empire to be educated as Romans; and the rest of the people encamped on Roman territory.

A LARGE GOLD MEDALLION OF VALENS

Then came trouble. The Visigoths were to be supplied with food, that is, they were to be allowed to buy it. The generals in command thought this an excellent opportunity to fill their purses. Therefore they provided the poorest and vilest of food, but charged an exorbitant price for it. The Goths were enraged, and they were not so helpless as the generals supposed, for it seems that at the crossing of the river many of the shrewd barbarians had bribed the Roman officers to allow them to retain their weapons. Before the Romans fully realized this, the Eastern Goths, or Os'tro-goths, also begged to be allowed to cross the Danube, for they, too, were pursued by the dreadful Huns. The emperor was thoroughly alarmed now, and he answered, "No." Nevertheless, the Ostrogoths came. The emperor was too frightened to dare to wait for a sufficient number of troops. He met the invaders in battle. The Roman army was destroyed and he was slain.

These Germans were jubilant. They had learned that they, whom the Romans looked upon as savages and barbarians, could overcome the famous legions. Matters were in their own hands. They marched on to the southward, plundering and destroying as they went, until they were very close to Constantinople.

Valens's nephew, who had become emperor in the West, was wise enough to see that he needed the help of a thoroughly efficient commander, and he appointed a Spaniard named The-o-do'si-us as emperor in the East. Theodosius eventually united the two parts of the empire into one, over which he ruled. Seeing that he could not drive the Germans out of the empire, he called them allies, paid them to defend the frontier, and treated them with respect, but settled them in districts as far apart as possible. Many of them became faithful friends of Rome. Others were restless and ambitious, and only waited for a leader to rebel against the power of the empire.

This leader was found in Al'a-ric. Under his command they pillaged Greece; then they fixed their eyes upon Rome. The great Theodosius was dead, and the realm was now in the hands of his two sons, Ar-ca'di-us in the East and Ho-no'-ri-us in the West. The guardian of Honorius was a general named Stil'i-cho. He himself was a German, for it was now nothing unusual for the best generals and statesmen in Rome to be of German blood. So skilful was Stilicho that by using both his wits and his weapons he managed to keep the Goths from sweeping over Italy. This was no easy task, especially as the people who lived near the boundaries had been so distressed by enormous taxes that they almost looked upon the Goths as deliverers and made little resistance to them. Honorius had fled for his life, but when once in a safe retreat, he had proclaimed that his breast had "never been susceptible of fear." After the danger was over, he went back to Rome

HONORIUS IN MILITARY DRESS

to celebrate the return of peace. Then this sagacious young man concluded that Stilicho would be so elated by his success that he probably would try to make himself emperor; and he put to death the only man who could resist the invaders.

As soon as Alaric learned of the death of Stilicho, he

marched into Italy and besieged Rome. It was forced to yield. Messengers hurried to Ra-ven′na where Honorius was amusing himself. "Rome has perished!" they cried.

ALARIC IN ROME

"Why, she was eating from my hand only an hour ago!" exclaimed the emperor; for he was taking so little interest in the fate of his empire that he thought "Rome" was his favorite hen, to whom he had given that name. Alaric loaded down his army with silks and jewels and gold and silver, but he did not destroy the city. He did not wish to seize it for his countrymen, for he planned to conquer Sicily, and then make a kingdom for them on the African shores. On reaching the southern point of Italy, he was taken ill and died. His followers turned aside a little river from its course and buried him in its bed. Then the captives who had been forced to do this work were slain, that no one might know where their chief was laid and do his body despite. The Goths did not attack Rome again, but concluded that it was wiser to keep on good terms with the Romans. So they left Italy, and settled on lands in the north of Spain and in southern France. Alaric had captured the sister of Honorius, and she became the wife of At′a-wulf, brother-in-law of the Gothic chieftain.

Rome was surrounded by enemies. She needed every soldier that she could summon, and even before Alaric captured Rome, she had called the legions home from Britain to help her defend her boundaries. Indeed, hardly any boundaries remained, so broken had they become by the flood of new and strange races that had burst through them.

A strange, horrible people had lately come down upon Europe, — the Huns, from whom the Goths had fled at the Danube. These people were from Asia. They were short and thick-set. They had big heads and swarthy faces, with small, deep-set eyes. Their noses were so short and broad that they were often said to have nostrils but not noses. At first the people of Europe had cried out in horror that they were not men but beasts; then they declared that they were the offspring of demons. Since defeating the Goths, they had become bolder than ever, and now they had a strong leader named At′ti-la. Under him they had fought their way into what is now Austria and Hungary. The Roman emperors in the East paid them tribute; but the time had come when tribute would not satisfy them, and they marched into Gaul, or what is now France, and attacked Or′le-ans. A large part of Gaul was in the hands of a vigorous German people called Franks. The Romans, nevertheless, looked upon the country as a province of the empire. At the time of the coming of the Huns, the Roman governor of this province was an able general named A-ë′ti-us. When the Huns attacked Orleans and the citizens were almost in despair, Aëtius and his army came to the rescue, and the city was saved.

Before this time, the Goths and Aëtius had been at swords' points; but now they forgot that they had ever been enemies; and Romans, Goths, and Franks joined their forces under Aëtius on the plain of Chalons[1] in 451 A. D. Attila was defeated. This was one of the fiercest battles ever known. It was also one of the most important. If the Huns had been victors, they would have ravaged the land with fire and sword. More than this, the heathen Huns and not the partly Christianized Goths would have become the strongest power in Europe, and the spread of civilization might have been delayed for scores of years, perhaps for centuries.

Attila was defeated but not subdued, and after a time of rest he set out for Italy. He captured A-qui-le′i-a, and some of its frightened people fled to a group of marshy islands. Their rough little settlement became in time the powerful and beautiful city of Ven′ice. The Huns spared Rome, but went away loaded with an immense ransom from the terrified city.

The Van′dals, however, a people nearly related to the Goths, were more greedy. Having wandered into Gaul, they had forced their way into Spain. From Spain they had

[1] Sha-long′.

LAST CENTURIES OF THE EMPIRE 231

crossed to Africa, and had overrun the country as far as Carthage. They became a tribe of pirates, not caring where the wind drove them, provided there was plunder at the end of their voyage. Now they attacked Rome. For two weeks they plundered the city. Then they sailed away with thirty thousand captives to be sold as slaves and their vessels loaded to the gunwales with the choicest treasures of Rome.

For more than half a century, ever since the death of Theodosius the Great in 395 A. D., the empire in the East had had one ruler and the empire in the West another. In the fifth century the Gothic soldiers demanded land in Italy for homes, and backed the demand with their swords. The emperor was a boy whose name was Romulus Augustus; but he has been nicknamed Au-gus'tu-lus, or the "little Augustus," because of the contrast between the greatness of the Augustus who established the empire and the weakness of this its last emperor. The Goths deposed him and made their leader O-do-a'cer ruler of Italy. Odoacer took the title, not of emperor, but of patrician, and always claimed to rule as the deputy of the emperor of the East. The year 476, the date of this event, is sometimes spoken of as that of the fall of the Roman empire in the West, because at this time it became only a province of the Roman emperor in the East.

This "fall" of the Roman empire in the West did not seem at the time a matter of any weight. There was still an emperor, only he lived in Constantinople instead of in Rome. The troops that he commanded were still called the troops of the empire. It was, however, in reality one of the most important events in history. If the power of Rome had continued, the tribes about her would have fallen under her sway instead of having opportunity to develop and become separate nations. Again, now that there was no emperor in Rome, the power of the bishop of Rome, the great city of the West, increased rapidly. Third, it opened the way for a remarkable Gothic leader, The-od'o-ric, afterwards called the Great, to bring the Ostrogoths into Italy and give to that land of many invasions a time of peace and quiet. He succeeded in making himself ruler of Italy. He governed by the old Roman laws; he encouraged education and building and religious progress. He defended the country, and gave the people a feeling of freedom and safety that had not prevailed in the land for more than three centuries.

In the other countries of western Europe there was much confusion. There were Goths of several tribes, and there were other peoples. There were pagans, Christians, and half-Christianized folks. Even within the Church itself, there were two parties. These warring nations had one aim: they all were eager to press upon Italy.

Meanwhile, the empire in the East served a most useful purpose, for it kept the tribes of Asia out of Europe. Sometimes they were driven back by the forces of the empire, sometimes they were bribed to depart; but, whether vanquished or bribed, they were kept in their own country, and thus Christianity and civilization in Europe, which they would have utterly overwhelmed, had a chance to develop. During the reign of Justinian his famous general Bel-i-sa'ri-us succeeded in recovering Africa, Sicily, and a part of Spain from the barbarians, and in driving the Goths out of Italy.

LAST CENTURIES OF THE EMPIRE 233

Before they yielded, they used the mausoleum of Hadrian as a fort. The massive, dignified structure became a clumsy fragment, and the exquisite statues were torn down and hurled upon the besiegers. Justinian is famous not only for the victories of his army but for the collection of Roman laws

THE EMPEROR JUSTINIAN

which he had made. The Romans were the greatest of lawmakers, and this priceless collection has been the basis of the codes of nearly all the chief states of the world.

In the seventh century, not only the empire in the East, but all southern Europe was threatened by the Turks. They were Mo-ham'med-ans, or followers of Mo-ham'med, an Arabian who declared that God had sent an angel to him to teach him a pure and true religion. After a little, he and his disciples began to force their belief upon the various tribes of Arabia at the point of the sword. After he died, his followers conquered Syria, Persia, Egypt, and Northern Africa. They had tried to capture Constantinople, but had failed. They overcame Spain and swept on into France, shouting their battle-cry, "There is one God, and Mohammed is his prophet!" From Spain they marched to the north across the Pyrenees and into France. The Mohammedans in the East were pressing upon Asia Minor and Constantinople; those in the West were already in France. It seemed entirely probable that both divisions might march toward Italy and thrust Christianity out of southern Europe.

Before doing that, however, they must overcome the Franks. These Franks had made rapid gains in political power. They held southern Gaul, Bur'gun-dy, and western Germany. They were strong and prosperous, and they were able to meet the invaders. In 732 the leader of the Franks, Charles Mar-tel', or *Charles the Hammer*, met the western division of the Mohammedan forces on the plain of Tours.[1] He overcame them, and they were driven back to the foot of the Pyrenees. So it was that Europe was saved.

A fervent belief in the religion of Christ had taken possession of all Europe, and as there was no longer any emperor in Rome, the Pope, as the head of the Christian Church, had become the chief power in Italy. The Pope and the Frankish kings had been on friendly terms for a long while, and whenever he needed help, he appealed to the king of the Franks. In the ninth century, a German tribe called the Lom'bards seized northern Italy; and the Pope sent for aid to Charles the Great, or Char'le-magne, the reigning sovereign. Char-

[1] Toor.

lemagne soon conquered them and was crowned with the iron crown of Lom'bar-dy. He had already begun to conquer the Saxons who lived on the Elbe and the lower Rhine; and before he died, his rule extended over France, part of Germany, northern Italy, and a little strip at the north of Spain. This busy warrior established schools for the boys of his kingdom, built churches and bridges, and even found time to collect the ancient songs of his race. Although he is called Charlemagne, the French for Charles the Great, the German "Karl der Grosse" would be a much better name for this German prince. In the year 800 A. D. the Pope crowned him as emperor. Before this, the

Puvis de Chavannes
CHARLES MARTEL RETURNING VICTORIOUS FROM THE BATTLE OF TOURS
(From a Painting in the Town Hall at Poitiers)

Pope and the emperor at Constantinople had disagreed, and now, instead of talking of the Roman empire in the East and in the West as if it were one, people spoke of the Western Empire and the Eastern Empire. This was correct, for they had really become two.

The custom continued of crowning the king of the Franks as Emperor of the Roman Empire; but it was an exceedingly shadowy empire. The vast expanse of land ruled by Rome in her flourishing days gradually broke up into separate countries, and the vast crowd of people developed into different nations. This slow process was the real "fall of the Western Empire."

The fall of the Eastern Empire is marked by a definite date, 1453, for in that year the Turks captured Constantinople, and even to this day it is the capital of the Turkish Empire.

Roman history is not a mere tale of conquest, revolution, triumph, and downfall; it is a wonder story of how a tiny kingdom grew to be the ruler of the world. The kingdom becomes a republic, the republic an empire. Nation after nation moves swiftly across the field of vision and disappears, either merged into the all-embracing empire which has taken the world for its province, or so completely destroyed as to be lost in the darkness of the things that are forgotten. There are wars and rumors of wars; there is a moment of peace, and therein occurs the birth of the Holy Child of Bethlehem, whose words are to teach mercy instead of cruelty, and pardon instead of vengeance.

The empire has vanished, but its laws are written on the

LAST CENTURIES OF THE EMPIRE

statute books of the world, its language is on the lips of many nations, its military camps have become flourishing cities, its roads are mighty avenues of progress, its very failures are valued lessons. This is the Roman wonder story. The mightiest panorama, the most marvelous pageant that the world has ever gazed upon is "the grandeur that was Rome."

SUMMARY

The Germans were continually breaking into the empire. The Visigoths were allowed to cross the Danube; but the attempt to deprive them of their arms failed. The Ostrogoths, too, crossed the Danube, defeated the Romans in battle, and pressed close to Constantinople. Theodosius became emperor in the East. He quieted the Goths; but, led by Alaric, they pillaged Greece, then captured Rome. Alaric died. The Huns under Attila were overcome by Aëtius and the Goths at Chalons. Later, Attila approached Rome, but was bribed to depart. Rome was plundered by the Vandals. Romulus "Augustulus" was the last emperor of Rome. In 476 A. D., Odoacer became ruler of the West. Theodoric the Great gave Italy a time of peace and quiet. In the other countries of Europe there was confusion. During the reign of Justinian as emperor in the East, Belisarius recovered much territory from the barbarians, and drove the Goths from Italy. Justinian collected the Roman laws. The Mohammedans won many victories, but were overcome at Tours in 732 A. D. by Charles Martel and the Franks. Charlemagne was crowned by the Pope in 800 A. D. as emperor. The real fall of the Western Empire was the breaking up of the empire into separate countries. The fall of the Eastern Empire was marked by the capture of Constantinople by the Turks in 1453 A. D.

Roman history is a wonder story of how a tiny kingdom became the ruler of the world. The Roman Empire has vanished, but its influence upon the laws, languages, and governments of the world will never disappear.

SUGGESTIONS FOR WRITTEN WORK

A boy tells of his first sight of a German.

A Visigoth tells how his people were treated by the Romans at the Danube.

Charlemagne writes home of his coronation.

INDEX

AB'A CUS, used by Roman schoolboys, 176.
Ac'ti um, defeat of Antonius off, 167.
Actor, an, picture, 111.
Ad ri at'ic Sea, beset by pirates, 79; 99; crossed by Cæsar, 157; Diocletian lives near the, 218.
Æ'diles, first chosen, 37; picture, 37.
Æ ge'an, Sea, 100.
Æm i li a'nus. See *Scipio, Publius Cornelius Æmilianus.*
Æ ne'as, flees from Troy to Italy, 1-2; flight of, picture, 1; hero of the *Æneid,* 177.
Æ ne'id, written by Virgil, 177; saved by Augustus, 178.
Æ'qui ans, raid the Roman lands, 44; 46; conquered by Cincinnatus, 46-48; 55.
A ë'ti us, drives the Huns from Orleans and routs them at Chalons, 230.
Africa, 59, 72, 73, 77, 87; Scipio in, 94-95; Cato visits, 104; name given to Carthage and its territories, 106; Marius collects troops in, 129-130; 138, 143; wild beasts brought from, 152; 159; ruled by Lepidus, 164; visited by Hadrian, 203; entered by the Vandals, 230-231; recovered by Belisarius, 232; 234.
Af ri ca'nus, name given to Scipio, 96.
A gra'ri an Law, of Spurius Cassius, 38, 49; of Tiberius Gracchus, 114-116.
A gric'o la, conquers Britain, 196-197; the wall of, 203.
A grip'pa, Me ne'ni us, the fable of, 36.
Ag rip pi'na, wife of Claudius, 187.
Al'a ric, pillages Greece, and besieges Rome, 227-228; in Rome, picture, 228; death and burial of, 228-229.
Al'ba Lon'ga, founded by Ascanius, 2; 12; destroyed by Tullus, 15.
Alban Lake, is drained, 49-50.
Albans, remove to Rome, 14-15.
Al ex an'der the Great, conquests of, 99; cloak of, worn by Pompey, 149; Cæsar gazes at statue of, 152-153.

Al ex an'dri a, 166.
Al'li a (river), defeat of the Romans at the, 51.
Alps (mountains) crossed by Hannibal, 85-87; 120.
A mu'li us, steals Numitor's kingdom, 2; is put to death, 3.
Amusements of the Romans, 110-113. See also *Games* and *Gladiators.*
Ancestors, honors due to, 65.
Ancient country house, picture, 173.
An'cus Mar'ti us, King of Rome, 15-16; 17, 18.
An dro ni'cus, Liv'i us, introduces the theatre into Rome, 110-111.
An ti'o chus, King of Syria, 100; overcome by the Romans, 101-102.
An to ni'nus, is adopted by Hadrian, receives the title of "Pius," 206; 207; picture, 207.
Antoninus, Marcus Au re'li us, is adopted by Antoninus Pius, 205; rules with Verus, is a student of Epictetus, 206-208; 209, 210; picture, 207.
An to'ni us, Marcus, at Pharsalus, 157; delivers Cæsar's funeral oration, with picture, 162; is defeated by Octavianus, 163; joins the Second Triumvirate, 163-164; defeats Brutus and Cassius at Philippi, meets Cleopatra, 165-166; is defeated by Octavianus off Actium and commits suicide, 167; 169.
Ap'en nines (mountains), Cæsar plans a road along the, 160.
A pol'lo, 49.
"Apostate, The," title given to Julian, 222.
Appian, historian, 149.
Ap'pi an Way, 70; picture, 213.
Appius Claudius. See *Claudius.*
A pu'li a, 89.
A qui le'i a, captured by Attila, 230.
Arabia, Mohammed in, 234.
Ar ca'di us, rules in the East, 227.

240 INDEX

Ar chi me'des, defends Syracuse, 91-93; picture, 92.
Arch of Hadrian, picture, 204.
Army, Roman, reformed by Servius, 19; becomes stronger than the senate, 125-126.
Army-leader in his mantle, picture, 23.
As ca'ni us, 1; rules in Latium and founds Alba Longa, 2.
Asia, Marius goes to, 122; cities of, yield to Mithridates, 127; Mithridates driven back into, 131; hopes to become ruler of, 144; Cæsar goes to, 159; under Diocletian, 216; the home of the Huns, 229; tribes kept out of Europe, 232.
Asia Minor, 1; ruled by Alexander, 99; 101; in the power of Rome, 102; Mithridates seizes Roman land in, 126; ruled by Rome, 220; robbed to beautify Constantinople, 221; pressed upon by the Mohammedans, 234.
A si at'i cus, 101.
Assembly of tribes, plebeian, wins the right to make laws, 41. See *Comitia centuriata* and *Comitia curiata*.
At'a wulf, marries the sister of Honorius, 229.
Athenians, yield to Sulla, 131.
Athens, attacked by Philip V, 100; taken by Sulla, 131; Hadrian completes a temple and an arch in, 203-204.
Athletic contests, become cruel, 111.
A'tri um, 62.
At'ti ca, overcome by Sulla, 131.
At'ti la, is driven from Orleans and defeated at Chalons, 229-230; captures Aquileia, 230.
Augur, interprets the will of the gods, at a marriage, 66-67; picture, 67.
August, named in honor of Augustus, 170.
Au gus'tan Age of Latin literature, 181.
Au gus'tu lus, 231.
Au gus'tus, Caius Julius Cæsar Octavianus, offices held by, 170; Pontifex maximus, picture, 170; refuses to enlarge the empire, 171; guards the rights of the provincials, 171-172; provides amusements for the Romans, 172; as a builder, 173; literature under, 176-181; saves the *Æneid*, 178; 179; chooses Tiberius as his successor, 182; 198, 199, 202, 216. See also *Octavianus*.
Augustus (plural Augusti), as a title, 215, 218.
Au re'li an, captures Palmyra, 213-214.
Aurelius, Marcus. See *Antoninus*.
Austria, entered by Attila, 229.
Av'en tine Hill, Remus watches for omens on the, 3; 33; site of Andronicus's theatre, 110.

BALLISTA, picture, 131.
Baltic Sea, 120.
Ba sil'i ca, 173.
Bau'cis, 180.
Bel i sa'ri us, recovers much land from the barbarians and drives the Goths out of Italy, 232.
Ben e ven'tum, Romans defeat Pyrrhus at, 60.
Bethlehem, 181, 236.
Bi thyn'i a, 102.
Black Sea, 100, 126, 202, 220.
Boc'chus, 127.
Borrowing in Rome, the danger of, 34-35.
Bos'pho rus (straits of), 216, 220.
Bren'nus, routed by the Romans, 53-54.
Bride, a Roman, picture, 68.
Brit'ain, visited by Cæsar, 153-154; Caligula sails for, 185; Claudius invades, 186; conquered by Agricola, 196-197; visited by Hadrian, 203; legions recalled from, 229.
Brun du'si um, Cæsar sails from, 157.
Bru'tus, kisses the earth, drives Tarquinius from Rome, 22-23; condemns his sons to death, with picture, 26.
Brutus, Marcus, pardoned by Cæsar, 158; conspires against Cæsar, 161-162; flees from Rome, 163; picture, 164; is defeated at Philippi and commits suicide, 165; Horace in the army of. 178.
Bugle player in Roman army, picture, 102.
Bur'gun dy, held by the Franks, 234.
By zan'ti um (Constantinople), is chosen by Constantine as his capital, 220.

CÆCUS, Appius Claudius, prevents peace with Pyrrhus, 59; 70.
Cæ'li an Hill, 32, 33.

INDEX

"Cæsar," as a title, 199, 215, 217.
Cæ'sar, Caius Ju'li us, refuses to divorce his wife, 134; favors Pompey's leadership in the third war with Mithridates, 143-144; would show mercy to Catiline, 147-148; becomes one of the First Triumvirate, 151-153; picture, 152; in Gaul, 153-154; leads the people's party, 154-155; crosses the Rubicon, with picture, 154-155; his kindness to his enemies, defeats Pompey's troops in Spain, 156; defeats Pompey at Pharsalus, 157-158; pardons Brutus, 158; punishes the murderers of Pompey, 158-159; favors Cleopatra, 159; honored by the senate, 159-160; his plans for ruling the world, 160-161; his assassination, 161; last moments of, picture, 161; funeral oration of, 162-163; the family of, extinct, 190; 216.
Cæsars, palace of the, 201.
Ca lig'u la, becomes emperor, 185-186; forms the prætorian guard, 185; 198.
Ca mil'lus, takes Falerii, 48-51; routs the Gauls, 53-54; 121.
Camillus, Lucius Fu'ri us, nephew of the Camillus who took Falerii, routs the Gauls, 55.
Campus Martius, 20, 47; visited by Marius, 128; porticoes of the, 173.
Can'næ, Romans defeated at, 89, 120.
Cape Saint Vincent, 171.
Capitol, 9; building of the, 17; saved by Marcus Manlius, 52-53; saved by Camillus, 54; 96; 127; catches fire, 132; trophies of Marius in the, 152; 173.
Capitoline Hill, 12, 17; cliffs of the, picture, 27; citadel built on the, 32; 33; 149; destruction of temple on the, 192.
Ca'pre æ, withdrawal of Tiberius to, 184.
Capri, 184. See *Capreæ*.
Captain, picture of a, 44.
Cap'u a, attacked by the Samnites, 55; 70; forms an alliance with Hannibal, 89-90; regained by the Romans, 93; Caius founds colony at, 117; 139.
Car a cal'la, admits to citizenship all that are freeborn, 211.
Ca rac'ta cus, captured and carried to Rome, 186-187.

Car'thage, early history of, 72-73; first war with Rome, 74-78; yields Sardinia and Corsica to Rome, 79; the soldiers of, 80; 81; in the Second Punic War, 80-95; 97, 102; visit of Cato to, 104; destroyed by Scipio, 104-106; 107, 111, 129; Cæsar plans to rebuild, 160; Æneas in, 177; Hadrian visits, 203; 231.
Car tha gin'i ans, opposed by Pyrrhus, 59; as merchants, 73; in the first Punic War, 76-78; overcome their revolting colonies, 80; in the Second Punic War, 80-95; 96, 100; attacked by Masinissa, 104; surrender to Rome, 106.
Carthaginian wars, losses and gains of Rome in the first two, 96-97; effect of victories upon the Romans, 109-114.
Carthaginian women, picture, 105.
Cas'sius, conspires against Cæsar, 161; is defeated at Philippi and commits suicide, 165.
Cassius, Spurius, proposes Agrarian Law, 38; 49.
Cas'tor, 31.
Catapult, picture, 132.
Cat i li'na, Lucius Ser'gi us, plots to overthrow the state, 146-148.
Cat'i line. See *Catilina*.
Ca'to, Marcus Por'ci us, censor, is sent to Carthage, 103-104; feelings of, toward his slaves, 113.
Cato, Marcus Porcius, descendant of Cato the censor, favors the death penalty for Catiline, opposes the recall of Pompey, 148; is made governor of Cyprus, 153; kills himself at Utica, 159.
Ca tul'lus, writes a satire against Cæsar, 156.
Cau'ca sus Mountains, 145.
Cau'dine Forks, defeat of the Romans at the, 57.
Censors, powers of the, 41-42.
Cha lons', Aëtius overcomes the Huns at, 230.
Chariot race, picture, 70.
Char'le magne, the extent of his rule, is crowned as emperor, 234-235.
Charles Martel, routs the Mohammedans at Tours, 234; picture, 235.

INDEX

"Charles the Hammer." See *Charles Martel.*
Children, the training of, 64-65.
Christ, the religion of, preached in Rome, 188.
Christianity, in Southern Europe endangered, 234.
Christian martyrs in the Colosseum, picture, 217.
Christians, persecuted by Nero, 188-189; by Domitian, 198; by Diocletian, 217; granted religious freedom by Constantine, 220; oppressed by Julian, 222; 232.
Cic'e ro, Marcus Tullius, prosecutes Verres, 142; denounces Catiline, with picture, 146-148; picture, 148; arouses enmity, 148-149; driven into exile, 153; the Philippics of, 163; proscription and murder of, 164.
Ci lic'i a, 143, 165.
Cim'bri, defeated by Marius, 120-121; 127; 223.
Cin cin na'tus, Lucius Quinc'ti us, conquers the Æquians, 46-48; 109, 136.
Cin'na, Lucius Cornelius, becomes consul with Marius, 129-130; 134, 137, 151.
Circus Maximus, 17, 69.
Citizen, Roman, the rights of a, under Augustus, 172.
Clau'di us, becomes emperor, invades Britain, frees Caractacus, 186-187; 198.
Claudius, Ap'pi us, decemvir, scorns the plebeians, 35-36; suicide of, 40-41.
Cle o pa'tra, becomes queen of Egypt, 159; meets Antonius in Cilicia, 165-166; fête at the court of, picture, 165; kills herself, 167.
Clients, 7, 8.
Clo a'ca Max'i ma, 17, 69; picture, 18.
Clu'si um, 27.
Clyde (river), Agricola's wall from the Forth to the, 197.
Cnæ'us Pom pe'i us, 135.
Colonies, influence of, 71.
Col os se'um, built by Vespasian, the ruins of, picture, 193; completed by Titus, 194; Christian martyrs in the, picture, 217.
Column and forum of Trajan, picture, 202.
Co mi'ti a cen tu ri a'ta, 20.
Co mi'ti a cu ri a'ta, 8.
Commentaries, of Cæsar, 154.

Com'mo dus, plays the part of gladiator, is called the "Roman Hercules," 210.
Con'stan tine, the vision of, with picture, 218-219; wins a victory at Milvian Bridge, publishes the Edict of Milan, chooses Byzantium for his capital, 220-221; strengthens the government, 221-222; arch of, picture, 221.
Con stan ti no'ple (Byzantium), chosen by Constantine as his capital, 220; approached by the Germans, 226; 231; the Mohammedans fail to capture, 234; taken by the Turks, 236.
Con stan ti'nus, 218. See *Constantine.*
Con stan'ti us, becomes Augustus, 218.
Consul with war cloak, picture, 137.
Consuls, appointed, 25; may be plebeians, 32.
Cor'inth, 100; destroyed by the Romans, 103; 111; Cæsar plans to rebuild, 160.
Co rin'thi ans, insult Roman envoys, 103.
Co ri o la'nus, Caius Mar'ci us, takes Corioli, 44; returns to the Volscians, 45-46; yields to his mother's prayers, picture, 46; 136.
Co ri'o li, taken by Caius Marcius, 44.
Cor ne'li a, and her "jewels," 114; picture, 115.
Cor'si ca, 73; yielded by Carthage to Rome, 79.
Cras'sus, Marcus, defeats the gladiators, becomes consul, 140; becomes one of the First Triumvirate, 151-153; is made consul, is slain, 154.
Cu'mæ, 22.
"Cunctator," 88, 94.
Cup of friendship, the, picture, 175.
Cu'ri æ, 7, 8.
Cu ri a'ti i, contest with the Horatii, 13-14; picture, 13.
Cyn os ceph'a læ, battle of, 100.
Cy'prus, governed by Cato, 153.

DA'CI ANs, revolt against Domitian, 197; refused tribute by Trajan, 202.
Dacian War, 202.
Dal ma' ti a, Diocletian withdraws to, 218.
Danube, 171; Marcus Aurelius near the, 207; 212, 220, 223, 224; crossed by the Goths, 226; 229.

INDEX

De cem'vi ri, are chosen, 39.
"Delight of mankind," name given to Titus, 125.
Del'phi, 22, 49.
De mos'the nes, 163.
Di a'na, 137.
Di o cle'ti an, becomes emperor, 214; chooses two Augusti and two Cæsars, 215; lives in splendor at Nicomedia, 216; persecutes the Christians, 217; withdraws to Dalmatia, failure of his plans of government, 218.
Do mi'ti an, celebration of his birthday, 166; as a commander, 196; picture, 197; drives away the philosophers, governs the provinces well, persecutes the Christians, is assassinated, 197-198; murderers of, not punished, 200; 201.
Drama, introduced by Livius Andronicus, 110-111.
Dru'sus, Marcus Livius, favors the Italians, 124.
Drusus, son of Tiberius, poisoned by Sejanus, 184.
Du il'li us, honors paid to, 77.
Dying Gaul, picture, 80.

EAGLE-BEARER in the Roman army, picture, 125.
East, the, changes in, 99; overcome by Rome, 102; the Romans imitate the ways of, 108; war with Mithridates in the, 126-127, 130-132; difficulties of Rome in the, 139; Pompey in the, 144, 146; Antonius rules in the, 164, 165; Germanicus sent to the, 184; 190; Trajan makes war in the, 202; Hadrian gives up land in the, 203; pestilence brought from the, 206; luxuries brought from the, 209; 220; Valens emperor in the, 225; Arcadius rules in the, 227; emperors in the, pay tribute to the Huns, 229; 231; empire in the, keeps out the Asiatic tribes, 232, is threatened by the Turks, 233; the Mohammedans in the, 234; 236.
Eastern Empire, fall of the, 236.
Eastern Goths, 226. See *Ostrogoths*.
E ge'ri a, appears to Numa, 11.
Egypt, ruled by Alexander, 99; 100; attacked by Philip V., 100; Pompey flees to, 158; Cæsar makes Cleopatra queen of, 159; 165, 166, 171; under Diocletian, 216; 234.
El'ba (island), 73.
Elbe (river), 171, 235.
Elephants, brought by Pyrrhus to Heraclea, 59; repulsed by the Romans, 77; taken across the Alps by Hannibal, 87; war-elephant, picture, 59.
Empire, map, ix.; weakness of the, 209-210; sold at auction, 210-211; in confusion, 212; pressing dangers of the, 215; is granted religious freedom by Constantine, 220; grows weaker and is divided, 225; is united by Theodosius, receives the Germans as allies, 226; is divided, 231; fall of the, 236.
Ep ic te'tus, philosopher, 198; Marcus Aurelius Antoninus, a student of, 207.
E pi'rus, 59; Pyrrhus returns to, 60; overcome by Sulla, 131.
Es'qui line (hill), 33.
E tru'ri a, 50; Marius collects troops in, 130; revolt in, 136; Catiline flees to, 147.
Etruscan city, gate of an, picture, 48.
E trus'cans, 13; Etruscan warrior, picture, 12; acknowledge Tarquinius Priscus as King, 17; aid Tarquinius Superbus, 31; Rome protects the Latins from the, 32; wars with the Romans, 48-51; 55; unite with the Samnites, 58; 75; athletic contests of the, 111.
Eu phra'tes River, Hadrian goes beyond the, 203.
Europe, the Huns come down upon, 229; 230; confusion in western part of, Christianity has a chance to develop in, 232; southern part of, threatened by the Turks, 233; saved by the Franks, 234.
Eux'ine (sea), 126. See *Black Sea*.

FA'BI US MAXIMUS, Quin'tus, Cunctator, story of, 62: "the delayer," 88-89, 92.
Fable, of Menenius Agrippa, 36.
Fa le'ri ans, surrender to Camillus, 51.
Fa le'ri i, falls into the hands of the Romans, 50-51; ravine below, picture, 50.
Farther Spain, 152. See *Lusitania*.

INDEX

Fasces, 17.

"Father of his Country," title given to Cicero, 148; title given to Cæsar, 160.

Faus'tu lus, 3.

Fawn, pet of Sertorius, 137-138.

First Triumvirate, 151-153.

"Five Good Emperors," the, 200-208.

Fla min'i an Way, 79.

Flam i ni'nus. Titus Quinctius, defeats Philip at Cynoscephalæ, 100; announces the victory at the Isthmian games, 100-101.

Fla'vi an amphitheatre, 193. See *Colosseum*.

Flora, festival in honor of, picture, 69.

Forth (river), Agricola's wall from the Clyde to the, 197.

Fo'rum, ruins of the, picture, 33; in the time of Nero, picture, 189; rebuilt by Vespasian, 192.

France, home of the Gauls, 49; 120; the Goths settle in, entered by the Huns, 229, by the Mohammedans, 234; ruled by Charlemagne, 235.

Franks, Gaul held by the, 230; aid in overcoming the Huns at Chalons, 230; overcome the Mohammedans at Tours, 234; assist the Pope, 234; 236.

Furies, live on the threshold, 68.

GA'BI I, deceived by Sextus, 22, 23.

Gal'ba, becomes emperor, 190; 198.

Ga le'ri us, opposes the Christians, 217; ends their persecution, 218.

Games, pleasing to the gods, 66. See *Isthmian*; picture, 135; the people demand, 172.

Gaul crossed by Hannibal, 87; ravaged by Cimbri and Teutones, 120; 139; in the hands of Cæsar, 153-154; Cæsar marches through, 155; Caligula plunders, 185; 190; Hadrian journeys through, 203; rebellion in, subdued by Diocletian, 217; entered by the Huns, 229; held by the Franks, entered by the Vandals, 230; 234.

Gauls, Etruscans attacked by the, 48-49, 51; enter Rome, but are driven away, 52-54; routed by Lucius Furius Camillus, 55; unite with the Samnites, 58; prepare to come down upon Rome, 79; buried alive, 79-80; dying Gaul, picture, 80; meet Hannibal, 84-85; join the Carthaginians, 87; suppressed by Vespasian, 191.

Geese of Juno, give warning, 52; picture, 53.

Gens, in early Rome, 6.

Ger man'i cus, loyalty of, 183; death of, 184; 186.

Germans, 184; push into the Roman lands, 212; description of the, 223-224; overcome the Roman army, 224-226; become allies of the Romans, 226. See *Goths, Visigoths*, and *Ostrogoths*.

Germany, western part of, held by the Franks, 234; under Charlemagne, 235.

Glad'i a tors, 111-113; going to the Circus, picture, 113; war with the, 139-140; price of, 152; under Augustus, 172; Commodus combats with the, 210.

Golden Age of Latin literature, 181.

Golden House of Nero, 190.

Goths, cross the Danube, 225; are repulsed by Stilicho, 227; settle in Spain and France, 229; aid in overcoming the Huns at Chalons, 230; depose Romulus Augustus, and make Odoacer ruler of Italy, 231; driven from Italy by Belisarius, 232. See *Germans, Visigoths* and *Ostrogoths*.

Grac'chus, Caius Sem pro'ni us, the land law of, 116-117; founds colonies, is slain, 117; 172.

Gracchus, Ti be'ri us, the land law of, 114-116.

Greece, coast cities of, attacked by pirates, 79; 99, 100, 101; in the power of Rome, 102; the Romans imitate the ways of, 108; Roman youth sent to, 108; Pompey flees to, 156; Cæsar starts for, 157; 167; Horace studies in, 178; ruled by Rome, 220; robbed to beautify Constantinople, 221; pillaged by Alaric, 227.

Greek, a, advises the Carthaginians, 77.

Greek, the language, 59; fashionable in Rome after the Punic Wars, 108, and during the reign of Augustus, 176.

Greeks, Troy captured by the, 1; 22; Etruscans beaten by the, 48; attempt to drive the Mamertines from Sicily, 73-74; 75; freed from piracy by the Romans, 79; 100, 101, 177, 203.

INDEX

HA'DRI AN, travels through the empire, builds a wall across England, completes in Athens a temple to Jupiter, 203-204; builds a mausoleum, 205; the mausoleum of, used as a fort, 233; arch of, picture, 204; mausoleum of, picture, 205.
Hadrian's Tomb, picture, 205.
Ha mil'car, in Spain, 80-81.
Han'ni bal, the oath of, leads the Carthaginian forces in Spain, 81; picture, 82; marches to the Adriatic Sea, 82-89; crossing the Alps, picture, 86; crossing the Rhone, picture, 88; is victorious at Cannæ, 89; winters in Capua, 89-90; meets misfortunes, 93; is recalled to Africa, 94; is routed at Zama, 95; is an able statesman, 96; 99, 100; death of, 101-102.
Has'dru bal, commands the Carthaginian forces, is slain, 81.
Hel'les pont, 101.
Her a cle'a, Pyrrhus victorious at, 59.
Her cu la'ne um, destroyed, 196.
Her'cu les, god of property and commerce, 65.
Her min'i us, opposes Porsena, 29.
Her'ni cans, allies of the Romans, 43-44.
Holy City, 191. See *Jerusalem*.
Holy of Holies, entered by Pompey, 145.
Ho'mer, poet, 185.
Ho no'ri us, rules in the West, slays Stilicho, 227; picture, 227; thinks. " Rome " was his hen, 228; the sister of, captured by Alaric, 229.
Houses of the early Romans, 62.
Horace, or Quintus Horatius Flac'cus, poet, 178-179.
Ho ra'ti i, contest with the Curiatii, with picture, 13-14.
Ho ra'ti us, consul, 41.
Horatius, keeps the bridge, with picture, 28-30.
Hungary, entered by Attila, 229.
Huns, the Visigoths flee from the, 224-225; the Ostrogoths flee from the, 226; description of the, 229; enter Austria, Hungary, and Gaul, 229; are driven from Orleans and routed at Chalons, 230; Rome is spared by the, 230.

I BE'RUS (river), crossed by Hannibal, 83.
Il lyr'i a, 79.
Imperator, title taken by Augustus, 169.
India, partly under rule of Alexander, 99.
I o'ni an Sea, beset by pirates, 79.
Ireland, Agricola plans to conquer, 197.
Isth'mi an games, 100.
Isthmus of Corinth, Cæsar plans a canal through the, 161.
Italians, ask Romans for aid, 74; become citizens, 124-125; slain by Mithridates, 126-127; slain by Sulla, 133.
Italy, Æneas in, 2; 33, 34, 44, 49; Rome becomes mistress of, 58-60; held by the Roman roads, 70; shape of, 72; 73, 74, 78; coast cities of, attacked by pirates, 79, 84; entered by Hannibal from the north, 87; 88, 89, 93, 96, 99, 100; sheep-raising in, 114; 115; in danger from the Cimbri and Teutones, 119-121; 123, 125, 129, 139, 143, 144, 145; 155; Cæsar marches through, 156; 171, 177, 189; 191; 206, 209; barbarians are charmed by, 224; protected from the Goths by Stilicho, 227; entered by Alaric, 227-228; the Goths depart from, Alaric dies in, 228-229; Attila sets out for, 230; Gothic soldiers demand land in, Odoacer becomes ruler of, 231; ruled by Theodoric, 232; Belisarius drives the Goths from, 232; the Pope becomes the chief power in, the Lombards seize northern, 234; under Charlemagne, 235.

JA NIC'U LUM (hill), 16; captured by Porsena, 28.
Ja'nus, the temple of, 12, 66, 181.
Je ru'sa lem, 124; taken by Pompey, 145; taken by Titus, with picture, 191-192; 195; colony founded on the site of, 205.
Jesus, the birth of, 181; crucifixion of, 185.
Jews, lose Jerusalem to Pompey, 145; lose Jerusalem to Titus, 191-192; burned by Titus, 195; persecuted by Domitian, 198; rebel against Hadrian, 205.
John, apostle, banished by Domitian, 198.
Jo se'phus, at the capture of Jerusalem, 192.
Ju dæ'a, subdued by Pompey, 145; 185; conquered by Titus, 191-192.

Ju gur'tha, conquest and death of, 117-118, 121; 127, 154.
"Jules Verne," 92.
Julia, daughter of Cæsar, 154.
Ju'li an, "the apostate," 222.
Ju'li us, name given to the fifth month of the Roman year, 160.
Julius, 198. See *Cæsar, Caius Julius.*
Juno, 52; wife of Jupiter, 65-66; picture, 66.
Ju'pi ter, temple of, 9; 11; destroys Tullus, 15; 16; Capitol built in honor of, 17; 36; father of the gods, 65; 66; the temple of, 147; 180, 204.
Justinian, 232; collects the laws of Rome, 233; picture, 233.
Ju've nal, poet, quotation from, 194.

"KARI DER GROSSE," the German name of Charlemagne, 235.
Kingdom of Rome, becomes a republic, 23.
Kings, the Roman, legends of, 1-23.

LAR'TI US, opposes Porsena, 29.
Latin, learned by conquered peoples, 71; despised by the Romans, 108; learned by Andronicus, 110; in Spain, 152.
Latins, aid Tarquinius, 31; found Rome, 32; refused land by the Romans, 38; allies of the Romans, 43-44; war with the, 55-57; treated by the Romans almost as equals, 78; 96, 99; refused the rights of Roman citizens, 117.
La'ti um, 2.
La vin'i a, 2.
La vin'i um, founded by Æneas, 2.
Legionary on the march, picture, 119.
Lep'i dus, consul, prepares to attack Rome, 137.
Lepidus, Marcus Æ mil'i us, son of the consul Lepidus, aids Antonius; joins the Second Triumvirate, 163-164; defeats Brutus and Cassius at Philippi, is dropped from the Second Triumvirate, 165.
Lictors, with picture, 17.
Light-armed soldier, picture, 156.
Light footman in Carthaginian army, picture, 83.

"Little Augustus," the, nickname of Romulus Augustus.
Lives, Plutarch's, 203.
Liv'y, or Titus Livius, historian, 92, 179-180, 185.
Lom'bards, are conquered by Charlemagne, 234-235.
Lom'bar dy, conquered by Charlemagne, 235.
Lu'ci us Tar quin'i us Pris'cus, goes to Rome, 16; King of Rome, 17-18.
Lucius Tarquinius Su-per'bus, becomes King of Rome, 20-21; buys the Sibylline Books, 21-22; fails to subdue the Gabii, 22; fears the punishment of the gods, 22; is driven from the throne, 23.
Lu cre'ti a, the death of, 23.
Lu cul'lus, Lucius Li cin'i us, rule of, in the East, 144-145.
Lu si ta'ni a, revolts against Rome, 137.
Lustrum, 20.

MAC E DO'NI A, 99, 100; in the power of Rome, 102; Cæsar enters, 157; 163, 164, 165.
Macedonians, 101.
Macedonian War, First, 100-101.
Ma'cra (river), limit of the Roman power, 60.
Mæ ce'nas, friend of literary men, 178, 179.
Mag ne'si a, overthrow of Antiochus at, 101.
Mam'er tine dungeons, 118.
Mam'er tines, ask Romans for aid, 74.
Ma nil'i an Law, 144.
Ma nil'i us, Caius, 143.
Man'li us, Mar'cus, saves the Capitol, 52-53; helps the plebeians, 54.
Manlius, Ti'tus, puts his son to death, 56.
Map, city of Rome, viii.; Roman Empire, ix.
Mar cel'lus, nephew of Augustus, mentioned in the *Æneid,* 177.
Ma'ri us, Caius, conquers Jugurtha, 118; the rise of, 118-119; defeats the barbarians, 121; ambition of, 121-122; picture, 122; returns from Asia, 123; overcomes the Italians, 124-125; 126, 127; is driven into exile, 128-129; returns to Rome, 130; death

INDEX

of, 130 ; 133, 134, 137, 138, 151 ; trophies of in the Capitol, 152 ; 156 ; defeats the Cimbri and Teutones, 223.

Marriage, between patricians and plebeians, 41 ; ceremonies of, 67–69.

Mars, 2 ; picture, 11 ; priests of, 11 ; 32 ; god of war, 65 ; 74.

Marseilles. See *Massilia.*

Mas i nis'sa, attacks Carthage, 103, 104.

Mas sil'i a, 142.

Mausoleum of Hadrian, 233.

Max en'ti us, claims the throne, 218 ; is overcome by Constantine at Milvian Bridge, 220.

Max im'i an, resigns the throne, 218.

Meals, of the Romans, 175–176.

Med i ter ra'ne an Sea, 48, 72, 73, 77 ; western part of, ruled by Rome, 79 ; crossed by Scipio, 94 ; 97, 99, 100 ; becomes a "Roman lake," 107 ; pirates of the, overcome by Pompey, 142–14 ; countries of the, 209.

Mercury, 180.

Mes sa'na, 74.

Mes si'na, 74. See *Messana.*

Met a mor'pho ses, of Ovid, 180–181.

Me tau'rus River, 93.

Mil'an, the Edict of, grants religious freedom, 220.

"Military tribune with consular power," office of, may be held by plebeians, 41.

Mi ner'va, goddess of wisdom, 66.

Mith ri da'tes, is conquered by the Romans, 126–127, 130–132 ; third war with the Romans, 142, 143–146 ; death of, 146 ; 149, 151 ; the son of, defeated by Cæsar at Zela, 159.

Mo ham'med, 233, 234.

Mo ham'me dans, conquests of the, 233–234 ; are repulsed at Tours, 234.

Mounted officer, picture, 21.

Mus, De'ci us, sacrifices himself for his country, 56.

NEP'TUNE, games in honor of, 4 ; god of the waters, 66.

Ne'ro, becomes emperor, 187–188 ; after the burning of Rome, picture, 187 ; persecutes the Christians, taught by Seneca, 188–189 ; Roman forum in the time of, picture, 189 ; house of, 189–190 ; takes his own life, 190 ; 198 ; picture, 190.

Ner'va, the reign of, 200–201.

Nic o me'di a, chosen as his capital by Diocletian, 216.

North Sea, 120.

Nu man'ti a, yields to Rome, 106–107.

Nu'ma Pom pil'i us, King of Rome, 10–12 ; 15 ; 32.

Nu mid'i a, 103, 117, 118.

Nu'mi tor, 2 ; regains his kingdom, 3.

OC'TA VI A'NUS, Caius Julius Cæsar, defeats Antonius, is made consul, joins the Second Triumvirate, 163–164 ; defeats Brutus and Cassius at Philippi, rules Rome and the West, 165 ; defeats Antonius off Actium and becomes ruler of the world, 167 ; takes the title of Imperator, 169, of Augustus, 170.

O do a'cer, made ruler of Italy by the Goths, 231.

"Op'ti mus," title given to Trajan, 201.

Or'le ans, besieged by the Huns, 229–230.

Os'ti a, founded, 16.

Os'tro goths, cross the Danube, overcome the Roman army, 226 ; brought into Italy by Theodoric, 232.

O'tho, becomes emperor, takes his own life, 190–191 ; 198.

Ov'id, Pub'li us O vid'i us Na'so, with picture, 180–181.

PAL'A TINE HILL, 2 ; Romulus watches for omens on the, 3–4 ; founds Rome on the, 4 ; 33 ; Roman homes on the, 174.

Palla, 64.

Pal my'ra, ruins at, picture, 212 ; captured by Aurelian, 213–214.

Pan'the on, picture, 172 ; 173.

Papyrus manuscript found at Herculaneum, picture, 194.

Pater, the head of a gens, 6.

Pat'mos, Saint John banished to, 198.

"Patrician," title taken by Odoacer, 231.

Pa tri'cians, in early Rome, 6–8.

Paul, apostle, 124.

Persecution of the Christians by Nero, 188, 189, by Domitian, 198 ; by Diocletian, 217, 218.

Per'seus, defeated at Pydna, 102.
Persia, ruled by Alexander, 99; becomes powerful, 212; 234.
Persians, Constantine moves nearer to the, 220; fought by Julian, 222; 223.
Per'ti nax, emperor of Rome, 210.
Phar'na ces, son of Mithridates, 146.
Phar sa'lus, battle of, 157.
Phi le'mon, 180.
Philip II, ruler of Macedonia, 99; Demosthenes's *Philippics* against, 163.
Philip V, ruler of Macedonia, defeated at Cynoscephalæ, 100-101; 102.
Phi lip'pi, Brutus and Cassius defeated at, 165.
Phi lip'pics, of Demosthenes and of Cicero, 163.
Phœ nic'i a, subdued by Pompey, 145.
Phœ nic'i ans, 74. See *Carthaginians*.
"Pi'us," title given to Marcus Antoninus, 205-206.
Ple be'ians, origin of the, 7-8; win their rights, 32-42; sufferings of the, in war, 34; secede to the Sacred Mountains, return to Rome, 35-36; tribunes appointed for, 36-37; the poverty of the, 37-38; gain the right to elect their own tribunes, demand written laws, 39; second secession to the Sacred Mt., 40; assembly of tribes of the, win the right to make laws, are allowed to marry among the patricians, may become "military tribunes with consular powers," 41; may become consuls, are full citizens, 42.
Plin'y, the elder, death of, 196.
Pliny, the younger, writes to Tacitus, 196; 197; Suetonius a friend of, 198; corresponds with Trajan, 202.
Plu'tarch, historian and biographer, 146; 202-203.
Pœ'ni, 74. See *Carthaginians*.
Pol'lux, 31.
Pom pe'i i, destruction of, picture, 195, 196.
Pom pe'i us, Cnæ'us, 138. See *Pompey*.
Pom'pey, is sent against Sertorius, 138; becomes consul, 140-141; clears the Mediterranean Sea of pirates, 143; commands the Roman forces in the third war with Mithridates, 143-146; picture, 145; 146, 148; the triumph of, 149; becomes one of the First Triumvirate, 151-153; is made consul and ruler of Spain, leads the party of the nobles, 154-155; flees to Greece, 156; repulses Cæsar in Macedonia, 156-157; is overcome by Cæsar at Pharsalus, 157-158; is slain in Egypt, 158-159; the sons of, revolt against Cæsar, 161; 165; Livy called a follower of, 179.
Pon'ti fex max'i mus, 12.
Pon'tine Marshes, Cæsar plans to drain the, 160.
Pon'ti us, Ga'vi us, rejects his father's advice, 57; is put to death, 58.
Pon'tus, 126; becomes a Roman province, 145.
Por'se na, Lars, attempts to conquer Rome, 27-30.
Portugal, 137, 171.
Prætorian guard, formed by Caligula, 186; refuses to protect Nero, 190; punishes the murderers of Domitian, 200-201; disbanded and a new one formed by Severus, 211.
Pub lil'i us, wins free election of tribunes for the plebeians, 39.
Pu'nic Wars, the first war, 74-78.
Pyd'na, defeat of Perseus at, 102.
Pyr'e nees (mountains) crossed by Hannibal, 83-84, 87; crossed by the Mohammedans, 234.
Pyr'rhus, aids the Tarentines and the Greek colonists, is routed by the Romans, 59-60.

QUIN TIL'I AN, given a salary by Vespasian, 192.
Quin ti'lis, changed to Julius, 160.
Quir'i nal (hill), 33.

RAM and tongs, picture, 91.
Ra ven'na, retreat of Honorius, 228.
Re gil'lus, Lake, battle of, 31.
Reg'u lus, patriotism of, 77-78; leaving home for Carthage, picture, 78.
Re'mus, 3-4, 10.
Republic, Rome becomes a, 23.
Rhe'a Syl'vi a, 2.
Rhe'gi um, seized by Spartacus, 140.

INDEX

Rhine (river), 163, 171, 183, 191, 201, 212, 223, 235.
Rhone (river) crossed by Hannibal, 84; 87.
Roads, built by the Romans, 69-71.
Roman cavalryman, picture, 157.
Roman citizenship, 124, 125.
Roman Empire, map, ix.
Roman forum in the time of Nero, picture, 189.
"Roman Hercules," the, title given to Commodus, 210.
Roman lady, picture, 64.
Roman soldier, with scale armor, picture, 19; picture, 35, 129; soldiers with shields, picture, 54.
"Rome," favorite hen of Honorius, 228.
Rome, city of, map, viii.
Rom'u lus, founds Rome, 3-4; seizes the Sabine women, 4; makes peace with the Sabines, 5; 6; death and prophecy of, 8-9; 10, 12, 68; prophecy of, 97; 121.
Romulus and Remus, the finding of, picture, 3; 32.
Romulus Augustus, last emperor of Rome, 231.
Ru'bi con (river), limit of the Roman power, 60; crossed by Cæsar, with picture, 155.

SA'BINES, women of, seized by the Romans, 4; make peace with the Romans, 5; women of the, stopping the fight, picture, 6; 10.
Sacred Mountain, secession of the plebeians to the, 36, 40.
Sacrifice, offering up a, picture, 15.
Sa gun'tum, besieged by Hannibal, 82.
Saint Angelo, Castle of, picture, 205. See also *Mausoleum of Hadrian*, 233.
Sa lo'na, Diocletian withdraws to, 218.
Sam'nite footman, picture, 57.
Sam ni'tes, attack Capua, 55; defeat the Romans at the Caudine Forks, 57; are subdued by the Romans, 58.
Sar din'i a, yielded by Carthage to Rome, 79; taken by Cæsar, 156.
Saxons, in the power of Charlemagne, 235.
Scaev'o la, Ca'i us Mu'ci us, holds his hand in the fire, with picture, 30-31; 136.

Schools, under Augustus, 176.
Scipio, Publius Cornelius, pursues Hannibal to the Rhone, is routed at the Ticinus, 87, and at the Trebia, 88.
Scipio, Publius Cornelius (Africanus), drives the Carthaginians from Spain, 93; in Africa, 94-95; triumph of, receives the name Africanus, 96; picture, 96; 101, 114; praises Marius, 118.
Scipio, Publius Cornelius Æmilianus (adopted by the son of Scipio Africanus), overcomes Carthage, 105-106.
Scotland, Agricola penetrates to, 196-197; 203.
Screen of shields, picture, 128.
Scrolls, writing utensils, and bookcase, picture, 179.
Sea fight, picture, 76.
Second Triumvirate, formation of the, 164.
Se ja'nus, attempts to become emperor, 184.
Senate, powers of the, 8.
Sen'e ca, teaches Nero, 188; is murdered by Nero, 190; 193.
Sen ti'num, Romans victorious at, 58.
Ser to'ri us, Quintus, leads the Lusitanians, 137-138; murder of, 138-139.
Se ve'rus, Alexander, emperor, 212.
Severus, Lucius Sep tim'i us, forms a new prætorian guard, 211.
Sex ti'lis, changed to August, 170.
Sex'ti us, son of Pompey, 165.
Sex'tus, deceives the Gabii, 22; insults Lucretia, 23.
Sheep-raising, 114.
Sibyl, sells the Sibylline Books to Tarquinius, 22-23.
Sib'yl line Books, 22; burning of the, 132.
Sicilians, prosecute Verres, 141-142.
Sicily, corn brought from, 45; Pyrrhus in, 59; 72, 73, 74; the first Punic War in, 74-75, 77-78; becomes a Roman province, 78-79; 80; revolt of the slaves in, 117, 122, 138, 140; rule of Verres in, 141; 143; taken by Cæsar, 156; Alaric plans to conquer, 228; recovered by Belisarius, 232.
Slave, picture, 106.
Slave market at Rome, picture, 109.

INDEX

Slaves, 7, 8; became cheap, 110; treatment of, 113-114; revolt in Sicily, 117, 122.
Slingers in Carthaginian army, picture, 74.
Social War, 124-125, 126, 127, 171.
Solway Firth, 203.
Spain, 73; Hamilcar in, 81; 87, 89, 93; belongs to Rome, 97; Scipio sent to, 106; 137, 138, 139, 140; Cæsar in, 152-153; governed by Pompey, 154; Cæsar conquers Pompey's troops in, 156; suppresses the revolt of Pompey's sons in, 160; 190; Hadrian visits, 203; the Goths settle in, 230; partly recovered by Belisarius, 232; overcome by the Mohammedans, 234; Charlemagne's power in, 235.
Spaniards, stand by the Romans, 93.
Spar'ta, 103.
Spar'ta cus, leads the gladiators, 139-140.
Standard-bearer, picture, 124.
Stil'i cho, protects Italy from the Goths, is slain by Honorius, 227.
Sti'lus, used by Roman schoolboys, 176.
Stola, 64.
Sue to'ni us, historian, 198.
Sul'la, Lucius Cornelius, is sent against Mithridates, 127-128, conquers Mithridates, 130-132; picture, 133; proscriptions of, 132-134; becomes dictator, 134; retirement and death of, 134-135; 136, 137, 138; fines the Asiatic peoples, 144; 151, 156.
Switzerland, 120.
Syr'a cuse, forms an alliance with Hannibal, 89-90; is captured by the Romans, 90-92.
Syr'i a, ruled by Alexander, 99; 100, 101; subdued by Pompey, 145; 171, 191, 211, 234.

TAC'I TUS, historian, 190; receives letter from Pliny the Younger, 196.
Ta'gus River, 81.
Tan'a quil, 16, 18.
Ta ren'tines, conquered by the Romans, 58-60; 62.
Ta ren'tum, taken by the Romans, 58-60; 110; colonies founded at, 117.
Tar pe'i a, betrays her country, 5.
Tarpeian Rock, 5, 9, 27.
Tar quin'i us Pris'cus, Lu'ci us, comes to Rome, 16; rule of, 17-18; death of, 18; 69.

Tarquinius (Superbus) attempts of, to regain his throne, 26-31; 34.
Tenth Legion, at Pharsalus, 157.
Ter'mi nus, the god of boundaries, 12.
Teu'to nes, defeated by Marius, 120-121; 127, 223.
Thap'sus, victory of Cæsar at, 159.
Theatre, of Andronicus, 110.
The od'o ric the Great, becomes ruler of Italy, 232.
The o do'si us, unites the two parts of the empire, 226; the death of, 227, 231.
Thes'sa ly, Cæsar withdraws to, 157.
Thirty Tyrants, claim the throne, 211.
Thrace, 139; under Diocletian, 216; entered by the Visigoths, 224-225.
Thracian gladiator, picture, 139.
" Thumbs down," picture, 112.
Ti'ber, River, 2, 16, 33, 44, 46, 48; Marius appears at the mouth of the, 130; 162.
Tiberius, succeeds Augustus, with picture, 181-182; opposition to, 183-184; withdraws to Capreæ, dies, 184-185; 198.
Ti ci'nus River, battle of the, 87-88.
Ti'gris River, Hadrian goes beyond the, 203.
Titus, conquers Judæa, 191-192; Jerusalem taken by, picture, 191; as a builder, 193-195; 196; 198, 199; arch of, picture, 196.
Toga, worn by the Romans, with picture, 63-64.
Tongs, for defense, picture, 91.
Tours, the battle of, 234.
Tower, used in siege of a town, picture, 90.
Tra'jan, picture, 205; becomes emperor, suppresses the Dacians, enlarges the empire, 201-202; column and forum of, picture, 202; enjoys literary men, 202.
Tras i me'nus, Lake, battle of, 88.
Tre'bi a River, battle of the, 88.
Tribes, 7.
Tribunes, for plebeians appointed, 36-37; right to elect given to plebeians, 39; allowed to sit at door of Senate house, 41.
Tri'remes, picture, 94; 95.
Triumph, a Roman, picture, 159.
Triumvirate, First, 151-153; Second, 164; Lepidus dropped from the, 165.
Trojans, 1.

INDEX

Troy, 1, 177.
Tullia, drives over the body of her father, with picture, 20-21.
Tul'li us, Ser'vi us, becomes King of Rome, 18-19; reforms of, 19-20; death of, 21; 34.
Tul'lus Hos til'i us, King of Rome, 12-15; destroyed by the gods, 15.
Turkish Empire, 236.
Turks, threaten Southern Europe, 233; capture Constantinople, 236.
Tus'can Sea, 143.
"Twelve Cæsars," 198, 200.
"Twelve Tables," the, 39.
Tyne River, 203.

URNS for ashes of the dead, picture, 178.
U'ti ca, besieged by Scipio Africanus, 94-95; becomes the leading city of Africa, 106; Cato kills himself at, 159.

VA'LENS, picture, 225; permits the Goths to enter Thrace, is slain by them in battle, 225-226.
Va le'ri an Law, 27.
Va le'ri o-Ho ra'tian Laws, passage of the, 41.
Va le'ri us (Lucius), consul, 41.
Valerius, Pub'li us, proposes the Valerian Law, 27.
Van'dals, enter Gaul, Spain, and Africa, and plunder Rome, 230-231.
Va'rus, loss of Roman army under, 172, 183, 184.
Ve'i i, captured by the Romans, 49-50; 53; Romans think of dwelling in, 54; 126.
Ven'ice, founded by fugitives from Aquileia, 230.
"Veni, vidi, vici," Cæsar's account of the battle of Zela, 159.
Ve'nus, goddess of beauty, 66; Cleopatra dressed as, 166.
Ver'res, the trial of, 141-142; 171.
Ve'rus, Lucius, adopted by Antoninus Pius, rules with Marcus Aurelius Antoninus, 205, 206.
Ves pa'si an, becomes emperor, 191; appreciates Quintilian, 192; as a builder, pardons Josephus, 192-193; 198.
Ves'ta, goddess of the hearth, 2, 65.
Vestal virgins, school of, picture, 65.
Ve su'vi us, Mount, the battle of, 56; eruption of, 196, 202.
Vi'a Ap'pi a, 70.
Victorious general thanking his army, picture, 95.
Vim'i nal (hill), 33.
Vintage festival, picture, 38.
Vir'gil, or Publius Vir gil'i us Ma'ro, poet, with picture, 176-178; 185.
Vir gin'i a, death of, with picture, 40.
Vis'i goths, are permitted to enter Thrace, overcome a Roman army, 224-226; approach Constantinople, 226.
Vi tel'li us, becomes emperor, is slain, 190-191; 198, 199.
Vol'sci ans, raid the Roman lands, lose Corioli, 44; are led by Coriolanus, 45-46; 55.

WEST, the, in the power of Rome, 102; difficulties of Rome in the, 139; Octavianus rules in the, 164; 225, 231; fall of the empire in the, 231; 232; the Mohammedans in the, 234; 236.
Western Empire, fall of the, 236.
Western Goths, 224. See *Visigoths.*
Women's court in the house of a wealthy Roman, picture, 174.
Worship, Roman, 66.

YOKE, Æquians sent under the, 47; Romans sent under the, at the Caudine Forks, 57; Roman army passing under the, with picture, 120.

ZA'MA, battle at, 95.
Ze'la, Cæsar defeats the son of Mithridates at, 159.
Ze no'bi a, is conquered by Aurelian, 213-214.

The Riverside Press
CAMBRIDGE . MASSACHUSETTS
U . S . A